THE ARKANSAS
CLASSIC COUNTRY
COOKBOOK

THE ARKANSAS
CLASSIC
COUNTRY
COOKBOOK

Traditional and Contemporary Recipes

Compiled and Tested by
Ruth Moore Malone
&
Bess Malone Lankford

August House Publishers, Inc.
LITTLE ROCK

Published by August House, Inc.,
P.O. Box 3223, Little Rock, Arkansas 72203,
501-372-5450.

Printed in the United States of America

10 9 8 7 6 5 4 3 2 1

LIBRARY OF CONGRESS CATALOGING-IN-PUBLICATION DATA

Ruth Moore Malone
Bess Malone Lankford
The Arkansas Classic Country Cookbook. / Ruth Moore Malone, Bess Malone Lankford.
1st ed.
p.   cm.
Includes index.
ISBN 0-87483-349-3 (pbk.: alk. paper) : $11.95
1. Cookery, American -- Southern style. 2. Cookery -- Arkansas.
I. Lankford, Bess Malone. II. Title.
TX715.2.S68M32 1994
641.5975--dc00   94-2744

First Edition, 1994

Executive editor: Ted Parkhurst
Design director: Ted Parkhurst
Cover design: Kitty Harvill, Harvill-Ross Studios
Text Illustrations: Wendell E. Hall

This book is printed on archival-quality paper that meets the
guidelines for performance and durability of the Committee on
Production Guidelines for Book Longevity of the
Council on Library Resources.

AUGUST HOUSE, INC.   PUBLISHERS   LITTLE ROCK

Contents

Beverages

Egg Chocolate

> 1 ounce semi-sweet chocolate
> 2 tablespoons sugar
> 1 cup milk
> 1 cup water
> 1 egg, separated

Grate chocolate and combine with sugar. Bring milk and water to a boil, stir in chocolate and sugar; simmer for 2 to 3 minutes, stirring constantly. Beat egg yolk until creamy. Beat egg white to a stiff froth. Pour boiling mixture over egg yolk and stir before serving in mugs or cups. Put a dollop of egg white on top of each serving. Serve very hot!
  Serves 2.

ðə ðə ðə

Eureka Eggnog

> 6 eggs, separated
> 6 tablespoons sugar
> 6 tablespoons bourbon or rum
> 1½ pints cream
> Freshly grated nutmeg

Beat egg yolks until light and gradually add sugar. Then blend in bourbon or rum. Beat egg whites until stiff and gently fold into first mixture. Stir in cream. Sprinkle each serving with nutmeg.
  Serves 6.

Wild Berry Milkshake

 1 cup fresh Arkansas berries
1¼ cups milk
  Dash salt
 1 pint vanilla ice cream

Wash berries, drain, and crush with a potato masher. Measure 1 cup and combine with milk, salt, and ¾ of the ice cream. Shake or beat until mixture is a smooth blend. Pour into glasses and top each with remaining ice cream and 1 or 2 whole berries. Serve immediately.
 Serves 4.

    🍃 🍃 🍃

Strawberry Leaf Tea

 ½ cup wild strawberry leaves
 2 cups boiling water
  Honey to taste

Wash strawberry leaves and steep in boiling water for about 3 minutes. Sweeten with honey. Serve hot or over ice.
 Wild leaf teas are best sweetened with honey because it is usually made from the nectar of wild flowers.
 Makes 2 cups.

Grape Cordial

2 pounds grapes
3 tablespoons powdered sugar
1 cup cold water

Wash grapes and drain. Mash and drain; or strain through cheese-cloth. Whisk grape juice, sugar, and cold water until sugar is dissolved. Add crushed ice just before serving.
Serves 4.

ᐤ   ᐤ   ᐤ

Peach Brandy

½ bushel peaches
15 pounds sugar (approximately)

Slice peaches and remove pits—do not peel. Layer peaches and sugar alternately in a 5-gallon crock until crock is full. Place a cloth on top and put in a cool place. When peaches begin to ferment, place a dinner plate weighted with a foil-covered brick on top—to make the juices rise to the top. Let stand for 4 to 6 weeks in a cool place.
After fermentation stops (there will be no more bubbling), strain through a cheesecloth and bottle.
Makes approximately 4 to 5 gallons.

Carrot Wine

   2   cups ground carrots
   2   quarts water
   5   cups sugar
1½   yeast cakes

Combine carrots, water, sugar, and 1 yeast cake in a large pan and boil for 1 hour. Remove from heat and strain. Stir remaining yeast into liquid. Pour into a jug or crock and cover tightly. Do not remove cover for 6 weeks. Then bottle, cork, and enjoy.

    Makes approximately 1 gallon.

❧   ❧   ❧

Dandelion Wine

   1   quart dandelion blossoms
   3   lemons
   2   oranges
   1   gallon boiling water
3½   pounds sugar

Pick dandelion blossoms after a rain and do not wash—water will wash away the pollen. Remove stems and place in a large container. Squeeze lemon and orange juice on top, adding the rinds. Cover with boiling water. Cover lightly with a thin cloth and let stand overnight.

    Strain through a fine sieve or cheesecloth and put in a crock. Stir in sugar. Cover with a thin cloth and let stand for several days, until fermenting almost stops—there will be little movement.

    Bottle and cork lightly until fermentation ceases; then seal.

    Makes approximately 1 gallon.

Grape Wine

1 gallon grapes
1 gallon honey
1 pound sugar

Wash grapes and drain. Place in a crock, cover with honey, and let stand for about 1 week.

Squeeze grapes through a cheesecloth. Pour sugar in bottom of crock and cover with grape juice. Cover crock and let grapes ferment. Check every week to see if fermentation has stopped—when the grapes no longer move.

Bottle, cork, and store in a cold dark place to age. Time depends on taste.

Makes about 1 gallon.

≈ ≈ ≈

Red Eye

3 ounces ice-cold tomato juice
Beer

Pour tomato juice into a 10- to 12-ounce glass. Fill with cold beer.
Serves 1.

Soups

Navy Bean Soup

2 cups dried navy pea beans
1 ham hock
2 large onions, diced
2 large carrots, diced
2 cloves garlic, minced

Wash beans in a colander. Soak overnight in water to cover. Drain the next day.

Place the ham hock in a large soup pot, adding beans, onions, carrots, and garlic. Cover with water (about 2 quarts) and bring to a boil. Reduce heat, cover, and simmer slowly for 3 hours or longer. Stir occasionally to loosen ham. Season to taste. Remove bone before ladling into soup bowls.

Serves 8.

❧ ❧ ❧

Cheese Soup

12 ounces Cheddar cheese
1½ tablespoons butter
1½ tablespoons flour
½ teaspoon dry mustard
1½ quarts milk
1 teaspoon salt
1½ tablespoons sherry
½ teaspoon Worcestershire sauce

Grate cheese. Melt butter in a large saucepan; blend in flour and mustard. Slowly add milk, stirring constantly. Bring to scalding heat (when bubbles form around edges of saucepan)—do not boil. Season with salt, add cheese, and stir until melted. Lower heat; blend in sherry and Worcestershire sauce.

Serves 6 to 8.

Confederate Chicken Soup

    1   quart chicken broth (homemade is best)
    ½   cup diced celery
    1   cup milk
        Salt and pepper to taste
    2   teaspoons flour

Simmer chicken broth and celery in a heavy soup pot until celery is tender. Gradually stir in milk. Season with salt and pepper. Scoop out ¼ cup broth and blend in flour; stir into hot soup to thicken. Garnish with minced parsley.
    Serves 4 to 6.

ва   ва   ва

Cream of Crawfish Soup

    2½ cups cooked crawfish
    4   cups milk
    4   tablespoons butter
    2   tablespoons flour
    1   pint cream
        Salt and pepper
    2   tablespoons sherry

Shred crawfish and combine with milk in a double boiler; simmer for 30 minutes.
    Melt butter in a large saucepan, stir in flour, then cream. Cook while stirring until thickened. Remove crawfish and milk from heat and stir into cream mixture. Season with salt and pepper. Add sherry just before serving.
    Serves 8 to 10.

Potato and Onion Soup

    4   medium-sized potatoes
    2   medium-sized onions
    1   quart chicken broth
    ½   cup butter
        Salt and pepper to taste

Dice potatoes and onions. Bring broth to a boil; reduce heat. Add potatoes and onions to broth and simmer until tender. Then stir in butter and season with salt and pepper to taste. Allow to simmer for an additional 15 to 20 minutes.
　　Serves 4 to 6.

ta   ta   ta

Pumpkin Soup in Country Jacket

    1   large pumpkin (carefully cut off top)
        Salted water
    2   tablespoons butter
    2   tablespoons flour
    ¼   cup sugar
    2   cups milk
        Pinch salt
    ½   pint cream
    2   ounces sherry

Remove pulp from inside the pumpkin and the lid. Discard seeds and stringy part. Cut in cubes to make 2 pounds. Boil pumpkin cubes in salted water until cooked. Drain and press the pulp through a sieve into a large saucepan.
　　Melt butter in another saucepan, adding flour, sugar, milk, and a pinch of salt. Cook until thickened. Stir into pumpkin and simmer for about 15 minutes.
　　Before serving, rinse the inside of the pumpkin shell with boiling water to warm the "tureen." Add cream and sherry to the soup and serve it from the pumpkin. Use the pumpkin top as a lid.
　　Serves 4 to 6.

Pink Tomato Soup

    6   medium-sized pink tomatoes (red will do)
    2   green onions, chopped
    2   tablespoons butter
    1   cup milk
    1   cup half and half
    1   cup cream
    ¼   teaspoon dill weed
    1   tablespoon sugar
        Salt and pepper to taste
        Sour cream

Peel tomatoes. Sauté onions in butter until soft. Put tomatoes and onions in a blender. Add milk, half and half, cream, dill weed, sugar, salt and pepper; blend until smooth. Chill.

Serve in soup bowls, topping each with a dollop of sour cream. Serves 8 to 10.

èa   èa   èa

Turnip Soup

    2   pounds white turnips
    ¼   cup butter
    ⅓   cup flour
    2½ pints chicken stock
    ½   cup milk
    2   egg yolks, beaten
        Salt and pepper
    ½   cup cream, whipped

Wash turnips, cutting off tops and bottoms. Pare and slice. Cook until tender in boiling water to cover. Drain and mash.

Melt butter in a large saucepan and blend in flour. Stir in chicken stock, milk, and egg yolks. Then stir in turnips; season with salt and pepper. Heat thoroughly. Serve in bowls, topping each with a dollop of whipped cream and a dash of paprika.

Serves 6 to 8.

Down-Home Vegetable Soup

        1   3- to 4-pound soup bone (beef shank)
            Salt
        1   cup diced celery
        1   cup diced carrots
        1   cup diced potatoes
      1½   cups chopped tomatoes
        4   green onions, sliced
        2   tablespoons chopped parsley
        1   turnip, peeled and diced
        ½   head cabbage, shredded
        ½   teaspoon sugar
        1   teaspoon paprika
        ½   teaspoon celery seed
        1   bay leaf

Place soup bone in a heavy kettle. Add cold water to cover and sprinkle with salt. Bring water to a boil, cover, reduce heat, and simmer 2 hours. Pour in more hot water, if necessary.

Stir in vegetables and seasonings. Continue simmering for at least another hour. When serving, cut meat from soup bone for each bowl.

Serves 8 to 10.

Salads

Wilted Watercress Salad

    2   quarts watercress
    2   slices bacon, diced
    1   teaspoon salt
    ⅛   teaspoon black pepper
    2   teaspoons sugar
    3   tablespoons vinegar
    ½   cup water
    2   boiled eggs, chopped

Wash, chop, and drain watercress. Fry bacon until crisp; drain and reserve hot drippings. Toss watercress, bacon, salt, pepper, sugar, vinegar, and water. Pour hot bacon drippings over salad and sprinkle with chopped eggs.
    Serves 6 to 8.

       ða   ða   ða

Caesar Salad

    1   head romaine lettuce, torn into ½-inch strips
    2   tablespoons grated parmesan cheese
    ¼   teaspoon black pepper
    1   egg, at room temperature
    8   anchovies
        Dash Worcestershire sauce
    ¼   teaspoon hot mustard
    5   ounces olive oil
    1   clove garlic, mashed
    3   ounces wine vinegar
    1   cup croutons

In a salad bowl, squeeze the juice of one lemon on lettuce, adding parmesan cheese and pepper. Break egg into salad and toss well.
    In a small bowl, make a paste of anchovies, stir in Worcestershire sauce, mustard, olive oil, garlic, and vinegar; chill over ice in a larger bowl. Toss salad with chilled dressing. Top with croutons.
    Serves 4 to 6.

Creamy Cole Slaw

- 1 firm young cabbage
- 1 teaspoon dry mustard
- 1 teaspoon salt
- 1 tablespoon sugar
- 1 tablespoon flour
- 2 eggs, beaten
- ¾ cup milk
- 2 tablespoons vinegar
- 2 tablespoons lemon juice
- 1 tablespoon butter

Remove outer leaves from cabbage and cut in quarters. With a sharp knife, slice very thin. Let stand in cold water for ½ hour.

Mix dry ingredients, eggs, and milk in a saucepan. Blend in vinegar and lemon juice; cook until thickened, stirring continuously. Remove from heat and stir in butter. Cool and then refrigerate.

Drain cabbage and mix with enough dressing to moisten.
Serves 8.

&. &. &.

Hot Slaw

- 1 medium-sized cabbage
- 1 cup vinegar
- 2 tablespoons butter
- 1 egg, beaten
- 2 teaspoons sugar
- 1 teaspoon dry mustard
- 1 teaspoon salt
  Pepper (optional)

Shred cabbage. Bring vinegar to a boil. Remove from heat and quickly stir in butter, egg, sugar, mustard, salt, and pepper. Pour over cabbage and cover with a tight fitting lid. Serve in 5 to 10 minutes.

Serves 6 to 8.

Marinated Cauliflower Salad

    1   head cauliflower
    3   medium-sized carrots, peeled
    2   stalks celery
    1   small onion
    1   cup salad oil
    1   cup cider vinegar
  1½   teaspoons garlic salt
  1½   teaspoons oregano
        Salt and pepper to taste

Break cauliflower into small florets. Cut carrots and celery on the bias. Slice onion in strips.

Prepare marinade by combining oil, vinegar, garlic salt, oregano, salt, and pepper. Toss vegetables in marinade, cover, and marinate in refrigerator at least 12 hours. Serve well chilled.

Serves 4 to 6.

♨ ♨ ♨

Hot Spinach Salad

    1   pound fresh spinach
    4   strips bacon
    ½   small onion, sliced thin
    2   tablespoons white wine
    2   teaspoons sugar
    4   tablespoons salad oil
    6   tablespoons white vinegar
        Juice of 1 large freshly squeezed orange

Wash spinach (removing any stems not usable) and dry leaves. Chill until crisp, then pull into small pieces.

Cook bacon until crisp; drain and dice. Heat with remaining ingredients and pour over spinach. Serve hot.

Serves 2 to 4.

Chicken Salad

2 whole chicken breasts
1 teaspoon salt
4 hard-boiled eggs, diced
1 cup chopped celery
  Mayonnaise (preferably homemade)
½ teaspoon dry mustard

Wipe chicken breasts and place in water to cover in a heavy pan. Season with salt. Bring water to a boil over high heat. Lower heat, cover, and simmer 1 to 1½ hours, until tender. Let cool in broth.

Remove skin and bones from cooked chicken and dice meat. Place in a bowl and toss with eggs and celery. Fold in mayonnaise to moisten, adding dry mustard to taste. Cover bowl and chill.

Serve on crisp lettuce leaves with a bit of mayonnaise on top. Serves 6 to 8.

🦐 🦐 🦐

Picnic Potato Salad

4 cups cooked, cooled, and cubed potatoes
¼ cup Italian salad dressing
1 cup chopped celery
2 hard-boiled eggs, chopped
1 cup mayonnaise
  Salt and pepper

Toss potatoes in salad dressing; cover and marinate in refrigerator. Then stir in celery and eggs. Bind with mayonnaise. Season with salt and pepper to taste. Serve chilled.

Serves 8 to 10.

Sliced Potato Salad

  7 cups peeled and sliced boiled potatoes
 ⅓ cup chopped chives
  1 teaspoon salt
     Dash pepper
  2 tablespoons grated onion
 ½ cup salad oil
  2 ounces white wine
 ½ cup chopped celery
 ½ cup sour cream
 ½ cup mayonnaise

Carefully combine potatoes, chives, salt, pepper, onion, and salad oil; chill. Separately blend wine, celery, sour cream, and mayonnaise; chill. Combine chilled mixtures.
    Serves 8 to 10.

∾   ∾   ∾

German Potato Salad

  6 potatoes, cooked
 ¼ cup minced onion
 ¼ cup minced parsley
     Salt and pepper
     Dash Worcestershire sauce
  4 strips bacon, cooked crisp
 ¼ to ½ cup white vinegar
 ¼ to ½ cup chicken broth, heated

Slice potatoes and spread in a frying pan. Sprinkle with onion and parsley; season with salt, pepper, and Worcestershire. Crumble bacon and stir into potatoes. Pour in vinegar and chicken broth. Heat thoroughly, taking care not to break potato slices. Serve warm.
    Serves 6 to 8.

Old-Fashioned Mashed Potato Salad

8 potatoes, peeled
  Salt and pepper
4 hard-boiled eggs
¼ cup minced green pepper
¼ cup minced green onion
1 teaspoon minced parsley
1 cup oil and vinegar salad dressing

Steam potatoes, drain, and mash. Season with salt and pepper. Chop 3 of the eggs and toss with potatoes. Add green pepper, onion, and parsley. Cool. Mix in about 1 cup salad dressing to moisten; chill.

Rub remaining egg through a sieve. Mound salad on lettuce leaves and garnish with sieved egg. Add more parsley for color, if desired.

Serves 8 to 12.

❧   ❧   ❧

Black Cherry Salad

1 20-ounce can pitted black cherries
1 tablespoon gelatin
  Pineapple juice
½ pound cream cheese, softened

Strain cherries and reserve juice. Pour ¼ cup cold cherry juice over gelatin; let stand for 5 minutes. Heat remaining cherry juice and enough pineapple juice to make 2 cups. Combine with gelatin mixture and strain over cherries. Pour into a ring mold and chill until firm.

Beat cream cheese and thin with pineapple juice to consistency of whipped cream. Unmold salad on lettuce leaves. Pile whipped cheese in center of salad.

Tomato Aspic

3½ cups canned tomatoes
1 teaspoon salt
½ teaspoon paprika
½ teaspoon sugar
2 tablespoons lemon juice
2 tablespoons chopped green onions
4 or 5 young celery ribs and leaves, chopped
⅛ teaspoon red pepper (optional)
2 tablespoons gelatin
½ cup cold water

Bring tomatoes to a boil in a large saucepan. Stir in salt, paprika, sugar, lemon juice, onions, celery, and red pepper; reduce heat, cover, and simmer 30 minutes.

Dissolve gelatin in cold water. Strain tomato mixture and blend in gelatin. Pour in a ring mold or individual molds. Refrigerate until firm and well chilled. Unmold on lettuce leaves. Top with mayonnaise, if desired.

Serves 8.

Salad Dressings

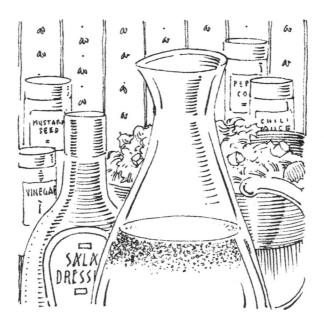

Sequoya Sour Cream Dressing

2 tablespoons sugar
1 teaspoon salt
1 teaspoon dry mustard
2 tablespoons lemon juice
2 tablespoons vinegar
1 cup sour cream

Blend sugar, salt, mustard, lemon juice, and vinegar. Place in a covered dish and refrigerate for 1 hour. Whip sour cream until light and stir in other ingredients. Serve on slaw or tossed salad.
    Makes about 1 pint.

ɜ.   ɜ.   ɜ.

Creamy Blue Cheese Dressing

¼ pound blue cheese
¼ pound cream cheese, softened
3 tablespoons cream
½ cup mayonnaise
    Dash salt and pepper
¼ teaspoon prepared mustard
¼ cup vinegar
6 tablespoons salad oil

Crumble blue cheese and set aside. Whip cream cheese and cream. Blend in remaining ingredients and beat until creamy. Gently stir in crumbled blue cheese. Refrigerate.
    Makes about 1 pint.

French Dressing

1   egg white
1   teaspoon dry mustard
1   teaspoon paprika
¼   cup vinegar
¼   cup lemon juice
1   clove garlic
1½ cups salad oil
1   teaspoon salt

Combine egg white, mustard, and paprika in a bowl and beat until thick. Pour in a quart jar and add remaining ingredients; shake until well blended.
     Makes about 1 pint.

      🙟   🙟   🙟

Tossed Salad Dressing

2   cups salad oil
½   cup tarragon vinegar
3   teaspoons salt
2   tablespoons sugar
2   teaspoons paprika
1   teaspoon dry mustard
1   teaspoon horseradish
2   teaspoons Worcestershire sauce
½   teaspoon coarsely ground pepper
1   teaspoon garlic juice (or 1 clove minced garlic)
2   teaspoons crushed sweet basil leaves

Put all ingredients (except basil leaves) in blender; buzz 10 seconds. Pour into a storage container and stir in basil leaves. Cover and store in refrigerator. Shake or stir thoroughly before serving.
     Makes about 1½ pints.

Honeybee Celery Seed Dressing

½ cup honey
1 teaspoon salt
1 teaspoon dry mustard
½ teaspoon paprika
1 tablespoon grated onion
⅓ cup vinegar
1 cup salad oil
1 tablespoon celery seed

Combine honey, salt, mustard, and paprika in a small mixing bowl. Blend in onion and a small amount of vinegar. Then, beat mixture, gradually adding salad oil and remaining vinegar. Stir in celery seed. This is especially good on fruit salad.

Makes about 1 pint.

⁂

Rose Petal Dressing

2 tablespoons rose petals
1 cup vinegar
2 tablespoons sugar
¼ teaspoon salt

Chop rose petals and cover with vinegar; let stand for a few minutes. Stir in sugar and salt; strain. Pour in a container and seal tightly. Refrigerate 24 hours. Serve over fruit salad.

Makes about 1 cup.

Breads

Baking Powder Biscuits

  2 cups flour
  ½ teaspoon salt
  2 teaspoons sugar
  4 teaspoons baking powder
  ½ teaspoon cream of tartar
  ½ cup shortening (scant)
  ⅔ cup milk

Sift dry ingredients into a bowl. Cut in shortening until mixture resembles coarse crumbs. Add milk, all at once, and stir just until dough follows fork around bowl. Pat or roll ½-inch thick on a floured board. Cut with a biscuit cutter. Place on a cookie sheet and bake in a 450° oven for 10 to 12 minutes.

  Makes 12 to 14 biscuits.

ᴤ   ᴤ   ᴤ

Sweet Potato Biscuits

  ¾ cup mashed sweet potatoes
  ½ cup milk
  4 tablespoons melted butter
  1¼ cups flour
  4 teaspoons baking powder
  1 tablespoon sugar
  ½ teaspoon salt

Mix sweet potatoes with milk and butter. Sift remaining ingredients and add to sweet potatoes, making a soft dough. Turn out on a floured board and toss lightly until outside looks smooth. Roll out ½-inch thick; cut with a floured biscuit cutter. Place on a cookie sheet and bake in a 450° oven for about 15 minutes.

  Makes 10 to 12 biscuits.

Squaw Bread

 2 cups flour
 2 teaspoons baking powder
 ¾ teaspoon salt
 1 cup milk (approximately)

Sift dry ingredients and stir in enough milk to form a biscuit dough. Roll ½-inch thick on a floured board. Cut in 2 x 3-inch shapes. Slit or cut holes in centers of dough. Fry in deep hot oil, turning only once. Bread should be crisp on the outside. Serve hot.
 Serves 8 to 10.

❧ ❧ ❧

Thoroughbred White Bread

 2½ cups lukewarm milk
 3 tablespoons sugar
 1 tablespoon salt
 2 yeast cakes
 2 tablespoons shortening
 7 to 7¼ cups flour

Mix milk, sugar, and salt in a large mixing bowl. Crumble in the yeast cakes and add shortening. Gradually work in flour; first mix with a spoon, then with hands, using the amount of flour necessary to make dough easy to handle. When the dough begins to leave the sides of the bowl, turn out on a lightly floured board to knead.
 To knead, fold dough over toward you, then press down away from you with heels of hands. Give dough a quarter turn and repeat until it is smooth, elastic, and does not stick to the board.
 Place dough in a greased bowl, turning once to bring greased side up. Cover with a damp cloth and let rise in a warm, draft-free place until double in bulk (1½ to 2 hours).
 Punch dough down and let rise again until almost double in bulk (35 to 40 minutes). Mold into 2 loaves and place in greased loaf pans. Bake in a 425° oven for 25 to 30 minutes.
 Makes 2 loaves.

River Road Rolls

½ cup butter
⅓ cup sugar
1 package plus ½ teaspoon dry yeast
1 egg
3 cups flour
  Melted butter

Let butter soften in a large bowl. Sprinkle with sugar; add ½ cup boiling water and let cool. Dissolve yeast in ½ cup warm water; beat in egg. Combine mixtures and stir in flour. Cover with foil and refrigerate overnight.

Roll out dough on a floured board and cut into circles; fold over. Place on a cookie sheet. Cover with a cloth and let rise in a warm place for about 2 hours.

Brush with melted butter and bake at 425° until golden brown, about 10 to 15 minutes. Serve immediately.

Makes about 20 rolls.

ૐ   ૐ   ૐ

Johnnycake

1 cup cornmeal
1 cup flour
1 teaspoon baking soda
3 tablespoons sugar
½ teaspoon baking powder
1¼ cups buttermilk
3 eggs, beaten
1 teaspoon salt
3 tablespoons shortening, melted

Sift dry ingredients; beat in buttermilk and eggs. Blend in salt and shortening. Pour into a preheated greased round pan. Bake at 350° for 25 to 30 minutes or until brown. Turn upside down on a hot platter and dot with butter. Serve immediately.

Serves 6.

Spoon Bread

 2 cups milk
 ½ cup cornmeal
 3 eggs, separated
 1 teaspoon baking powder
 ½ teaspoon sugar
 2 tablespoons butter, melted
 1 teaspoon salt

Heat milk to boiling point. Then stir in cornmeal and cook 5 minutes, stirring constantly. Remove from heat and cool slightly.

Beat egg yolks and add to cornmeal, along with baking powder, sugar, melted butter, and salt. Beat egg whites until stiff and fold into mixture. Pour into a shallow greased baking dish and bake in a 400° oven for 30 minutes. (Try freshly ground buhr cornmeal for a special treat.)

Serves 4 to 6.

🦐　🦐　🦐

Spider Cornbread

 1 egg
 1¾ cups milk
 2 tablespoons sugar
 ¾ cup cornmeal
 ½ cup flour
 1 teaspoon salt
 2 teaspoons baking powder
 1 tablespoon shortening

Beat egg and add 1 cup of milk. Sift sugar, cornmeal, flour, salt, and baking powder. Stir into egg mixture. Melt shortening in an iron skillet. Spoon in batter and pour remaining ¾ cup milk on top, but do not stir. Bake in a 375° oven for about 25 minutes. There should be a line of custard through the bread, hence its name.

Serves 6.

Hush Puppies

Long ago, while tall tales were told around campfires after a day's hunt, hounds would rest on the outer circle of the fire. When talking ceased for a moment, the low whine of a hound could be heard and its owner would toss a bit of corn pone and say, "hush, puppy." This delicious bit of cornbread succeeded in quieting the hound, so a new name was given to this cornmeal treat.

> 2 cups yellow cornmeal
> 2 teaspoons baking powder
> 1 teaspoon salt
> 2 tablespoons grated onion
> 1 cup milk, scalded
> 1 egg, beaten

Sift dry ingredients. Stir in onion and scalded milk. (To scald milk, simply heat in a saucepan until bubbles appear at edges.) Blend in egg. Shape in finger lengths or drop by spoonfuls into a deep fat fryer; fry until golden brown.

Drain on absorbent paper.

ʚ⃠   ʚ⃠   ʚ⃠

Crackling Bread

Cracklings are crisp bits of pork fat that remain after rendering.

> 1 cup cracklings
> 1 cup hot water
> 2 cups cornmeal
> 1 teaspoon salt

Break cracklings into small pieces and pour over ½ cup hot water to soften. Sift cornmeal and salt; add to cracklings. Add remaining hot water to make a dough.

Form into 2 large pones (oblong shapes) and place on a greased shallow pan. Bake in a 400° oven until golden brown, about 20 to 30 minutes.

Serves 8 or more.

Miniature Popovers

    1   egg
   ½ cup milk
   ½ cup flour

Stir all ingredients until combined, but not necessarily smooth. Pour into miniature teflon muffin tins; fill ½ full. Place in a cold oven, set temperature at 450°, and bake for about 25 to 30 minutes. Do not open oven during cooking time.

    Makes 12 miniature popovers.

ðŋ   ðŋ   ðŋ

Banana Nut Bread

   3 ripe bananas
   1 cup sugar
   1 cup shortening
   2 eggs, beaten
   2 cups flour
   1 teaspoon baking soda
   ½ cup broken nuts

Mash bananas. Cream sugar and shortening; combine with bananas and eggs. Sift flour and soda; stir into first mixture. Gently mix in nuts. Pour into a greased loaf pan and place in a cold oven. Set temperature at 325° and bake for 1 to 1¼ hours.

    Makes 1 loaf.

Molasses Bread

2½ cups sifted flour
2 teaspoons baking powder
1 teaspoon baking soda
1 teaspoon cinnamon
1 egg
½ cup sugar
½ cup molasses
¼ cup shortening, melted
1 teaspoon grated lemon rind
¾ cup buttermilk

Sift flour, baking powder, soda, and cinnamon in a bowl. Beat egg until light, adding sugar, molasses, shortening, and lemon rind. Add flour mixture to egg mixture alternately with buttermilk. Pour into a loaf pan and bake in a 350° oven for about 1 hour.

Makes 1 loaf.

❧   ❧   ❧

Huckleberry Muffins

1 cup huckleberries
2 cups flour
½ cup sugar
4 teaspoons baking powder
½ teaspoon salt
1 egg, beaten
1 cup milk
¾ cup butter, melted

Wash huckleberries and drain. Sift dry ingredients. Blend egg with milk and melted butter; add to dry ingredients, mixing only enough to dampen flour. Carefully stir in berries. Fill muffin tins ⅔ full. Bake in a 425° oven for 25 to 30 minutes.

Makes 12 muffins.

Razorback Ears

    1   cup flour
    ¼   teaspoon salt
    ¼ to ½ cup water
    1   cup sorghum

Sift flour and salt into a small bowl; stir in enough water to make a stiff dough. Divide dough into 10 to 12 portions; roll out as thin as possible on a floured board. Drop into deep hot oil. To make the "ear," twist each portion with a long-handled fork. Fry until brown; drain.

Boil sorghum until it forms a soft ball when dropped in cold water (234° to 236°). Dunk "ears" to glaze.

Makes 10 to 12.

Hot Cakes, Waffles,
French Toast

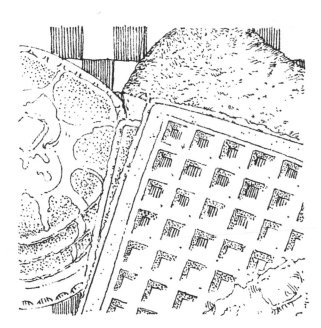

Flannel Cakes

2 cups sifted flour
1 teaspoon salt
3 teaspoons baking powder
2 eggs, separated
2 cups milk
1 tablespoon melted butter

Sift flour, salt, and baking powder. Beat egg yolks, adding milk and melted butter. Beat in flour mixture. Beat egg whites until stiff; fold into batter. Cook on a hot griddle until golden brown on both sides. Serve with plenty of melted butter and syrup.

Makes about 12.

જ&   જ&   જ&

Hot Cakes

1 egg
1 tablespoon melted butter
1 cup flour
1 cup milk
1 tablespoon sugar
1 tablespoon baking powder
¼ teaspoon salt

Beat all ingredients into a thin batter. Drop by ¼-cupfuls on hot griddle. Cook until golden brown on both sides. Serve immediately with butter and syrup.

Makes 6 to 8 hot cakes.

Huckleberry Hot Cakes

- 1 cup huckleberries (fresh or frozen)
- ½ cup water
- 1 egg
- 1 cup flour
- ¾ cup milk
- 2 teaspoons baking powder
- 2 tablespoons sugar
- ½ teaspoon salt
- 2 tablespoons melted butter
- 1 teaspoon vanilla

Place huckleberries in a saucepan with water. Bring to a boil and cook for 5 minutes. Remove from heat and strain.

Beat egg and mix in remaining ingredients. Carefully fold in huckleberries last. Cook hot cakes on a hot griddle, turning when bubbles form. Serve with melted butter and syrup.

Makes 6 to 8.

❧   ❧   ❧

Silver Dollar Pancakes

- 1 cup milk
- 2 tablespoons melted butter
- 2 eggs, beaten
- ½ teaspoon salt
- 2 tablespoons sugar
- 2½ teaspoons baking powder
- 1½ cups sifted flour

Combine milk, butter, and eggs in a bowl. Sift dry ingredients and blend mixtures, all at once. Add more milk, if necessary, to make batter the consistency of cream.

Pour pancakes the size of silver dollars on a hot griddle. Turn when pancakes are full of bubbles. When brown on both sides, serve with a choice of syrups.

Makes about 24.

Sweet Potato Griddlecakes

1½ cups sifted flour
3½ teaspoons baking powder
 1 teaspoon salt
 ½ teaspoon nutmeg
1¼ cups mashed cooked sweet potatoes
 ¼ cup melted butter
 2 eggs, beaten
1½ cups milk

Sift flour, baking powder, salt, and nutmeg. Combine remaining ingredients. Add to dry ingredients, mixing only until blended. Pour batter on a hot griddle and brown on both sides. Serve with Ozark honey.
    Makes about 10.

Pancake Sandwiches

6 pancakes
6 strips bacon
2 tablespoons butter
2 eggs

Prepare pancakes and keep warm. Fry bacon until crisp, but not dry; drain. Melt butter in a skillet over low heat. Break eggs, one at a time, into a saucer and slip into butter. Cook slowly until desired doneness, spooning hot butter over them so the whites will be set.
    Stack 1 pancake, 3 strips bacon, another pancake, 1 egg, and top with another pancake. Serve with syrup, if desired.
    Serves 2.

Buttermilk Waffles

       3   eggs, separated
   1½   teaspoons sugar
       ½   cup cooking oil
       1   cup buttermilk
       2   cups flour
       ½   teaspoon baking powder
       ½   teaspoon baking soda
       ½   teaspoon salt

Beat egg whites until stiff, gradually adding sugar. Whisk egg yolks until creamy, adding cooking oil and buttermilk; sift in dry ingredients and then beat well. Gently fold in beaten egg whites— do not beat. Cook in a hot waffle iron.

Makes 5 to 6 waffles.

&a   &a   &a

Whole Wheat Waffles

   1¼   cups whole wheat flour
       3   teaspoons baking powder
       ½   teaspoon salt
       ¼   cup sugar
       1   cup milk
       2   eggs, well beaten
       ⅓   cup melted butter, cooled

Mix flour, baking powder, salt, and sugar. Then stir in milk and eggs. Add butter and beat for a few minutes. Cook in a hot waffle iron.

Servings depend on size of waffle iron.

French Toast

6   ½-inch slices homemade or bakery bread
2   eggs, beaten
2   tablespoons powdered sugar
    Pinch salt
¼   cup cream
¼   teaspoon vanilla

Trim crusts from bread and cut in halves, diagonally. Mix eggs, powdered sugar, salt, cream, and vanilla; soak bread in mixture. Grill on a buttered griddle until golden on each side. Sprinkle with more powdered sugar. Serve with Ozark honey.
    Serves 4.

Fish

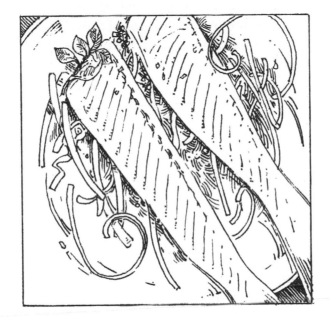

Beer Battered Fish

    3 to 4 pounds fish, cleaned
    2   beaten eggs
    12 ounces beer
    1   teaspoon salt
    1   tablespoon paprika
        Flour

Wash fish and pat dry. Combine eggs, beer, salt, paprika, and enough flour to make a medium-thick batter. Dip fish in batter and drain in a colander. Then deep-fry fish until brown and done—about 5 to 8 minutes, depending on size of fish. Drain on absorbent paper. Serve with lemon wedges and tartar sauce.

    2 to 3 servings a pound.

ໄ   ໄ   ໄ

Baked Fish with Stuffing

    3 to 4 pounds whole fish
    1   clove garlic
    4   tablespoons butter, softened
    ½   cup hot milk
    2   cups soft bread crumbs
    1   cup minced celery
    2   tablespoons minced onion
    1   tablespoon minced parsley
        Salt
        Juice of 1 lemon
        Paprika

Lay fish in a pan of cold water and thoroughly wash cavities; wipe dry. Rub cavities with garlic. Combine butter, milk, bread crumbs, celery, onion, and parsley. Stuff mixture into fish cavities; tie with string. Place in a buttered casserole. Sprinkle with salt, lemon juice, and paprika. Bake in a 375° oven for 1 hour.

    Serves 6 to 8.

Fisherman's Catch Marguery

A local version of an old French classic using fillets of bass, trout, or catfish.

1	pound fish fillets (bass, trout, or catfish)
1	tablespoon butter
1	cup minced onion
½	pound mushrooms, sliced
1	tablespoon flour
1	cup cream
	Salt and pepper
1	tablespoon chopped parsley
1	bay leaf
1	pound shrimp, cooked and cleaned
2	boiled eggs, chopped
½	cup grated cheese

Bring fillets to a boil in water to cover. Cook 2 minutes; remove from heat. Melt butter in a large saucepan and cook onion and mushrooms until limp. Stir in flour—do not let brown. Carefully add cream so it will not lump. Add salt and pepper to taste. Stir in parsley, bay leaf, shrimp, and eggs.

Arrange fillets in a baking dish and pour sauce over all. Sprinkle with grated cheese. Bake in a 350° oven just until cheese melts and bubbles form around the edges. Serve at once.

Serves 4 to 6.

Fish in Foil

6   fish fillets
6   tomato slices
2   tablespoons minced onion
2   tablespoons minced parsley
2   tablespoons olive oil
    Salt and pepper

Place each fillet on a piece of foil. Top with a tomato slice, onion, and parsley. Drizzle with olive oil. Season with salt and pepper.

Seal foil and arrange on a baking sheet. Bake in a 400° oven for about 20 to 25 minutes.

Serves 6.

ða   ða   ða

Grilled Fish in Corn Husks

4¼   pounds fresh fish fillets
     Salt and pepper
     Juice of 1 lemon
2   tablespoons minced pimentos
4   large ears of corn with husks
4   6-inch pieces of string
1   cup shredded mozzarella cheese
4   tablespoons butter, diced

Season fillets with salt and pepper; marinate in a mixture of lemon juice and pimentos. Carefully pull husks from corn, removing corn and silk—save corn for another use. Place husks and string in water to cover.

Remove corn husks from water and pat dry. Carefully place a fish fillet in each corn husk, folding if necessary. Equally divide cheese, butter, and pimento mixture over each fillet. Totally enclose fillets in husks and tie with string.

Place husks on charcoal grill and cook about 20 minutes, turning occasionally. Separate husks slightly with a fork to test fish for doneness. Serve in husks with lemon wedges.

Serves 4.

Catfish Fry

Catfish, fillets or small whole
Buttermilk
Yellow cornmeal
Cooking oil

Wash fish and pat dry. Soak in buttermilk and coat with cornmeal—dipping catfish in flour is blasphemy!

OUTDOORS: Fill an iron kettle ½ full with cooking oil; heat until sizzling over a campfire. Fry fish until golden—do not crowd. For an added treat, fry slices of bread along with fish.

INDOORS: Heat ¼-inch cooking oil in a heavy frying pan. Fry fish until golden on both sides, turning only once with a spatula. Test for doneness with a fork—if it flakes, it's done.

Serve immediately with hushpuppies and tartar sauce.

ès   ès   ès

Catfish Amandine

4   whole catfish (individual serving size)
Flour
Salt
½   cup butter
½   teaspoon onion juice
¼   cup finely slivered blanched almonds
1   tablespoon lemon juice
Parsley

Wash fish and dry well. Dust lightly with flour seasoned with salt. Heat half of the butter and onion juice in a heavy skillet. Sauté fish until light brown and flakes with a fork. Remove and place on a heated serving dish.

Pour drippings from skillet and add remaining butter with almonds and lemon juice; brown almonds slowly. When mixture foams, pour over fish. Garnish with parsley.

Serves 4.

Baked Catfish

    4   small catfish (for individual servings)
    ¼   cup lemon juice
    2   tablespoons Worcestershire sauce
    ¼   cup barbecue sauce
        Salt and pepper
        Flour

Clean fish, wash well, and pat dry. Score with cuts 1 to 1½ inches apart. Rub lemon juice and sauces into fish. Season with salt and pepper; coat with flour.

Place in a greased shallow baking dish and bake for about 1½ hours in a 350° oven, or until fish flakes when tested with a fork. This baking time is for fish weighing around 2 pounds—for smaller fish, adjust time.

Serves 4.

ஜ   ஜ   ஜ

Catfish Gumbo

    3   pounds catfish fillets
    2   pounds fresh okra
    2   tablespoons butter
    2   tablespoons flour
    1   cup chopped onion
    ½   green pepper, chopped
    2   cloves garlic, minced
    1½ cups canned tomatoes
    2   quarts water
        Salt and pepper to taste

Cut catfish into bite-size pieces. Thinly slice okra. Melt butter in a large pan and brown flour to make a roux. Add onion, green pepper, and garlic, stirring constantly. Slowly blend in tomatoes and water. Then stir in catfish and okra. Cover and simmer slowly for about 2 hours. Season with salt and pepper. Serve over rice.

Serves 8 to 10.

Ozark Blue Trout

The success of blue trout depends on freshness and leaving the natural film undisturbed.

      2 fresh trout
    ¼ cup tarragon vinegar
      2 cups water
         Juice of ½ lemon
    ½ teaspoon salt
    ½ bay leaf
      1 clove
      2 peppercorns
    ¼ cup chopped onion
    ¼ cup chopped carrot
    ¼ cup chopped celery

Clean fish but do not wash; handle as little as possible.

Combine remaining ingredients in a stewpan and bring to a boil. Reduce heat and let simmer for 20 minutes. Strain broth and return to stewpan. Return to a boil, reduce heat; plunge trout into broth and simmer (uncovered) until trout turn blue—about 5 to 10 minutes.

Remove from liquid and serve immediately with melted butter. Blue Trout is also delicious served cold with mayonnaise.

Serves 2.

Rainbow Trout Amandine

 6 trout fillets
    Salt and pepper
    Flour
 ¼ cup olive oil
 ½ cup butter
 ½ cup slivered almonds
    Juice of 1 lemon

Sprinkle fillets with salt and pepper; dredge in flour. Sauté in olive oil until delicately browned on each side. Arrange in a shallow baking dish.

Melt butter in a saucepan; stir in almonds and lemon juice. Pour over fillets. Bake in a 400° oven for 5 to 10 minutes, or until almonds are browned and fish flakes.

Serves 6.

 & & &

Sautéed Trout with Watercress Butter

 6 trout
    Milk
    Flour
    Salt and pepper
    Cooking oil
 4 tablespoons butter
 ¼ cup chopped watercress
 ½ teaspoon Tabasco sauce

Clean trout and remove fins; leave heads and tails on. Dip trout in milk and roll in seasoned flour. Heat cooking oil in a skillet and brown trout on both sides. When fish flakes with a fork, drain on absorbent paper.

Melt butter in a small saucepan; stir in watercress and Tabasco. Serve over trout. Garnish with lemon wedges.

Serves 6.

Stuffed Trout

 2 1-pound trout
 6 mushrooms
 1 leek
 1 carrot
 ¼ celery root (celeriac)
 4 tablespoons butter
    Salt
 2 eggs, beaten
 8 ounces port
 2 tablespoons flour
 ½ cup cream

Cut along back of trout to remove backbones and insides.

Thinly slice mushrooms, leek, carrot, and celery root. Sauté vegetables in 2 tablespoons butter until slightly softened. Season with salt to taste. Bind with eggs.

Stuff trout with vegetable mixture and place in a buttered casserole. Pour wine into the casserole and simmer over low heat about 8 to 10 minutes, or until trout is done. Gently lift out trout and carefully remove the skin. Thicken mixture left in casserole with a paste of flour and remaining butter. Add fresh cream and stir until thickened. Pour over trout.

Serves 2.

ðø ðø ðø

Arkansas Style Frog Legs

 1 pound frog legs (4 to 6 pairs per pound)
    Salted water
 2 cups buttermilk
 2 cups seasoned flour

Soak frog legs in salted water for 2 hours; drain. Dip frog legs in buttermilk and roll in seasoned flour. Deep-fry for 7 to 8 minutes. Do not crowd. Fry 2 to 3 pairs at a time. Drain and serve immediately.

Serves 2.

Beef

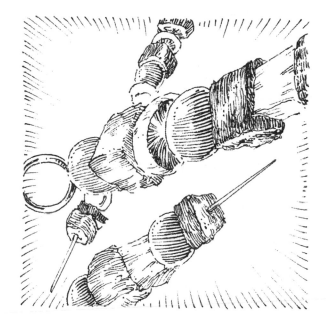

Roast Prime Rib

1 prime rib of beef
Seasoning salt
Rock salt

Sprinkle roast with seasoning salt. Cover bottom of roasting pan with 1 inch of rock salt. Place roast in center of pan; cover with rock salt. Insert meat thermometer in center of roast and cook to desired doneness in a 400° oven.

Rock salt provides even heat and a delicious flavor. Knock rock salt from roast before carving.

≈   ≈   ≈

Beef Stroganoff

1 pound beef tenderloin (or leftover roast prime rib)
4 tablespoons butter
1 teaspoon olive oil
2 tablespoons chopped green onions
½ pound mushrooms, sliced
¼ to ½ cup white wine
Dash Worcestershire sauce
8 ounces sour cream
Salt and pepper
Noodles

Slice meat into very thin strips. Heat butter and olive oil in a skillet until it sizzles. Add meat and stir until just delicately brown. Strain meat from pan.

Lower heat, add onions and mushrooms; sauté until barely limp. Stir in wine and Worcestershire sauce; simmer 1 minute.

Return meat to pan. Reduce heat again before adding sour cream to avoid curdling. Stir until all is heated through. Season with salt and pepper to taste. Serve over noodles and top with minced parsley.

Serves 4.

Steak on a Stick

  3   pounds beef tenderloin
  2   cloves garlic, crushed
1½   teaspoons salt
  2   cups olive oil
  1   cup tarragon vinegar
1½   teaspoons black pepper, freshly ground
  ⅛   teaspoon marjoram
  ⅛   teaspoon oregano
  3   bay leaves
  1   teaspoon paprika
  ¼   lemon, sliced thin
  ¼   cup chopped onion
36   mushroom caps
  1   pound bacon, cut in 1-inch slices
  6   ounces Roquefort cheese, crumbled

Cut beef into 30 1½-inch cubes. Make a marinade of garlic, salt, olive oil, vinegar, pepper, marjoram, oregano, bay leaves, paprika, lemon, and onion; blend well. Toss in meat, cover, and refrigerate overnight.

Arrange mushrooms, beef, and bacon on skewers, using 5 beef chunks on each. Broil over charcoal or under broiler—about 10 minutes for medium. Carefully coat each with 1 ounce of cheese and return to heat until cheese melts—about 1 minute.

Serves 6.

Smackover Sirloin

1 pound ground sirloin
2 slices Cheddar cheese
4 slices bacon

Form meat into 4 flat patties. Place cheese slice between 2 patties and seal meat together. Wrap bacon around each, fillet-style, and secure with toothpicks. Grill over charcoal until desired doneness.
   Serves 2.

ટ&   ટ&   ટ&

Little Switzerland Steak

1½ pounds round steak
     Flour
  2 cloves garlic, minced
  1 teaspoon salt
  ½ teaspoon pepper
  3 tablespoons butter
  2 onions, sliced
  1 pint beer

Trim fat from steak. Liberally sprinkle with flour and ½ of minced garlic, salt, and pepper; pound into meat with a mallet. Turn meat and repeat on other side.
   Heat butter in a large heavy skillet. Add meat and sizzle until brown on one side. Turn, adding more butter if necessary. Add onions and any remaining flour mixture. Pour beer over top and stir to loosen any particles in bottom of pan. Reduce heat, cover skillet, and simmer for about 1½ to 2 hours.
   Serves 4.

Braised Short Ribs

6 pounds lean short ribs
  Flour
  Salt and pepper
2 tablespoons butter
1 cup chopped carrots
1 cup chopped onions
½ teaspoon minced garlic
¼ teaspoon thyme
1½ cups water
2 bay leaves

Cut ribs into serving-size pieces. Coat with flour and season with salt and pepper. Place in a shallow roasting pan and brown in a 500° oven for 15 to 20 minutes. Watch carefully!

Melt butter in a large casserole. Stir in carrots, onions, garlic, and thyme; cook slowly until vegetables are tender. Spread mixture over bottom of casserole and arrange browned ribs on top.

Heat roasting pan on top of stove, add water, and stir to loosen particles where meat was cooked. Pour over meat. Add bay leaves, cover, and place in a 325° oven for 1 to 2 hours.

Serves 6 to 8.

જ   જ   જ

Leftover Stew

2 pounds leftover beef or lamb roast
¼ cup butter
2 onions, diced
1 cup diced carrots
1 cup diced celery
1 tablespoon Worcestershire sauce
2 teaspoons salt
¼ teaspoon pepper
¼ teaspoon paprika
3 to 4 cups water, broth, or leftover gravy

Cut meat into cubes. Heat butter in a stewpan and sauté meat and onions until lightly brown. Add vegetables, seasonings, and liquid. Cover and simmer for 1 hour.

Serves 6 to 8.

≈   ≈   ≈

Miner's Stew

1½ pounds boneless chuck, cut in 2-inch cubes
3   tablespoons flour
2   teaspoons salt
⅛   teaspoon paprika
⅛   teaspoon pepper
3   tablespoons cooking oil or bacon drippings
¼   cup chopped celery
½   cup chopped onion
½   tablespoon minced parsley
1   pint beef stock
⅓   cup tomato purée
1   cup peeled and diced potatoes
½   cup sliced carrots

Toss meat in a mixture of flour, salt, paprika, and pepper. Heat cooking oil in a heavy skillet and brown meat on all sides. Remove meat and place in a casserole.

Add celery, onion, and parsley to same skillet and sauté lightly—do not brown. Add beef stock and tomato purée; bring to a boil and pour over meat. Cover and cook in a 325° oven until meat is tender—about 1½ hours.

Separately simmer potatoes and carrots in water to cover for ¾ hour or until tender; drain. Add to stew and cook an additional hour.

Serves 6 to 8.

Cherokee Slumgullion

3 medium-sized onions, chopped
1 cup diced celery
2 tablespoons butter
1½ pounds ground beef
1 12-ounce bottle chili sauce
1 tablespoon vinegar
1 tablespoon Worcestershire sauce
1½ teaspoons salt
1 teaspoon brown sugar
1 teaspoon chili powder

Sauté onions and celery in butter in a large saucepan; brown lightly. Add ground meat and brown while mixing in remaining ingredients; cover. Simmer for 1 hour.

Serves 6 to 8.

ka   ka   ka

Maverick Meat Loaf

1 pound ground beef
6 bacon slices (4 minced, 2 halved)
1 egg, slightly beaten
½ cup milk
2 tablespoons melted butter
2 tablespoons catsup
2 tablespoons minced green onions
½ cup soft breadcrumbs

Combine ground beef, minced bacon, egg, milk, melted butter, catsup, onions, and breadcrumbs; toss with a fork. Pack one-half of mixture into a loaf tin. Place Cheddar cheese strips end to end in center of meat. Mold rest of meat mixture over cheese, covering completely. Arrange bacon slices on top.

Place in a cold oven, set temperature at 350° and bake for 1 hour—longer for a very well done meat loaf.

Serves 4 to 6.

Moro Meatballs

1 pound ground beef
½ pound ground pork
¼ cup flour
1 teaspoon salt
½ teaspoon pepper
½ cup grated onion
2 eggs
1 cup milk
 Margarine

Combine beef and pork in a mixing bowl. Add flour, salt, pepper, and grated onion. Stir in eggs, one at a time. Then add milk. Form into meatballs and fry in margarine until brown on all sides and cooked through.

Servings depend on size of meatballs.

Whistle Stop Chili

1 15-ounce can pinto beans
1 quart water
3 large onions, sliced
4 tablespoons cooking oil
1 pound ground beef
1 tablespoon salt
1 teaspoon chili powder

Place beans and water in a large saucepan and bring to a boil; simmer while preparing meat.

Fry onions lightly in cooking oil until brown; strain out. Sauté meat in remaining cooking oil until brown. Season with salt and chili powder. Add to beans and simmer for 30 minutes. Add more hot water if necessary.

Serves 6.

Blue Ribbon Veal Cutlets

- 4 2-ounce veal cutlets
- 2 slices Swiss cheese
- 2 thin ham slices
- ¼ cup flour
- 1 egg, beaten
- ¼ cup bread crumbs
   Salt and pepper
- ¼ cup butter
- 8 asparagus tips, cooked

Flatten veal. Place a slice of cheese and a slice of ham on 2 cutlets. Cover with other 2 cutlets and seal edges. Coat with flour, dip in egg, and roll in bread crumbs. Season with salt and pepper.

Heat butter in a skillet and sauté until golden brown on both sides. Top with asparagus.

Serves 2.

᪣ ᪣ ᪣

Calves' Liver and Onions

- 2 slices calves' liver
   Seasoned flour
- 4 tablespoons butter
- 1 onion, sliced thin

Dredge calves' liver in seasoned flour. Sizzle butter in a frying pan and quickly sauté liver. Reduce heat, add onions, and sauté until onions are slightly brown.

Serve immediately with pan drippings on top.

Serves 2.

Pork and Ham

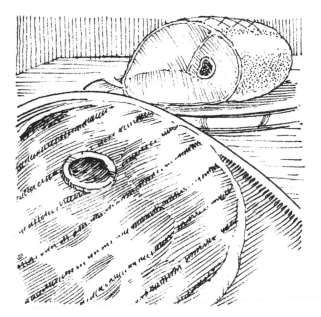

Old Tavern Pork Pie

1½ pounds lean pork, cubed
½ bay leaf, crushed
1 cup sliced carrots
½ cup sliced celery
½ cup finely chopped onion
4 cups hot water
    Salt and pepper, to taste
3 cooking apples, pared and sliced thin
3 tablespoons flour
¼ cup cold water
    Sweet Potato Biscuits (see page 32)

Combine pork, bay leaf, carrots, celery, onion, and hot water in a saucepan on top of stove. Season with salt and pepper. Cover and simmer until meat is tender. Drain and reserve 2½ to 3 cups of liquid.

Alternate layers of pork mixture and apples in a deep baking dish. Make a paste of flour and cold water; add to reserved liquid and thicken on top of stove. Pour over pork and apples. Place in a 350° oven while preparing Sweet Potato Biscuits.

Arrange unbaked biscuits over top of pork and return to oven, increasing temperature to 450°. Bake about 20 minutes or until brown on top.

Serves 6 to 8.

Red Flannel Pork Chops

4   pork chops
½   teaspoon dry mustard
¼   cup water
¼   cup vinegar
    Pinch red pepper
¼   teaspoon Tabasco sauce
3   tablespoons catsup
2   teaspoons Worcestershire sauce

Season pork chops with salt and pepper. Smear chops with dry mustard and place in a casserole.

Make a basting sauce of water, vinegar, red pepper, Tabasco, catsup, and Worcestershire sauce. Baste chops with sauce at intervals while baking for 1½ to 2 hours in a 300° oven.

Serves 4.

❦   ❦   ❦

Barbecued Baby Back Ribs

2   racks baby back ribs
8   thin slices lemon
1   cup chopped onion
½   cup catsup
1½   teaspoons Worcestershire sauce
½   teaspoon chili powder
    Dash Tabasco
1   cup water

Wipe ribs with a damp cloth and place on foil. Top each rack with 4 lemon slices. Tightly seal foil and place on a baking sheet. Cook in a 300° oven for 1½ hours.

Combine remaining ingredients in a saucepan and simmer until onions are tender. Discard lemons from ribs. Place meaty side down over charcoal until golden brown and crusty; turn and baste with sauce. Serve with remaining sauce on the side.

Serves 2 to 4.

Barbecued Spareribs

 1 rack of spareribs
 4 tablespoons brown sugar
 1 tablespoon celery seed
 1 teaspoon salt
 1 tablespoon chili powder
 1 teaspoon paprika
 1 6-ounce can tomato paste
1½ cups vinegar

Roll ribs in mixture of brown sugar, celery seed, salt, chili powder, and paprika. Place under broiler until light brown.

Then place in a shallow pan. Combine tomato paste and vinegar; pour over ribs. Bake in a 350° oven for 1 to 1½ hours, basting frequently.

Serves 1 to 2.

ɜ፝ ɜ፝ ɜ፝

Country Cured Ham

Wash and brush a country ham. Place skin side up in a large stewpan. Add enough water to cover ham. Cover pan and boil slowly—15 minutes for each pound of ham.

Then place ham in a shallow pan. Remove skin and let it drop around ham. Place in a 275° oven and bake for 1 to 1½ hours. Serve hot or cold.

Servings depend on size of ham.

Country Cured Ham and Red Eye Gravy

Country cured Arkansas ham is a real treat. In olden days, wild razorback hogs were often used. Today, there are many excellent places to obtain Arkansas country cured hams and bacon.

1 slice country cured ham
½ cup water
½ cup strong black coffee

Heat a heavy skillet and grease lightly with ham fat. Place ham in skillet and cook quickly; sear on both sides, turning only once. Do not overcook, but if slice is thick, add a little water to let ham cook without browning too much. Remove ham to a hot serving plate.

Add water and coffee to skillet, stirring up drippings. Pour over ham.

Serves 1 or 2.

&ea; &ea; &ea;

Ham Smothered with Sweet Potatoes

1 ham steak
2 sweet potatoes, sliced
2 tablespoons sugar
1 cup hot water

Brown ham slightly on both sides in a hot frying pan. Place in a baking dish and top with sweet potatoes; sprinkle with sugar. Add hot water to drippings left in frying pan and pour over ham and sweet potatoes. Cover and bake in a 350° oven until sweet potatoes are done and ham is tender. Baste occasionally with gravy. Just before serving, remove the lid and let top brown.

Serves 3 to 4.

White Beans and Ham

1   pound large dried navy beans
1   2-pound cured ham shank
1   teaspoon salt
1   teaspoon sugar

Cover beans with cold water, bring to a boil, and boil gently for 1½ hours. Trim fat from ham before adding to beans along with salt and sugar; simmer for an additional 1½ hours. Stir occasionally.
   Serves 6 to 8.

ع.   ع.   ع.

Ham Balls

½   pound ground cured ham
½   pound lean ground pork
½   cup milk
1   egg, beaten
1   slice bread, broken in pieces
¼   cup water
¼   cup vinegar
½   teaspoon dry mustard
½   cup brown sugar

Combine ham, pork, milk, egg, and bread. Shape into balls the size of eggs. Place in a greased baking dish.
   Make a syrup in a saucepan with water, vinegar, mustard, and brown sugar; pour over ham balls. Cook in a 325° oven for 1½ hours, basting often.
   Serves 6.

Holly Grove Ham Biscuits

½   pound cured ham
2   cups sifted flour
1   tablespoon baking powder
1   teaspoon Arkansas honey
½   cup water

Shred ham—fat, too. Combine flour, baking powder, and honey; blend in ham. Add enough water (at room temperature) to make a soft dough. No shortening is needed if fat is left on ham. Roll out on a floured board and cut with a biscuit cutter. Place on a baking sheet and cook for about 15 minutes in a 425° oven.

Makes 6 to 8 biscuits.

Poultry

Stagecoach Stop Chicken and Dressing

  1 plump chicken and giblets
  1 quart water
  4 tablespoons butter
  3 tablespoons flour
  ½ teaspoon salt
  2 tablespoons flour
  2 tablespoons milk
  2 hard-boiled eggs, chopped

Wash chicken and pat dry. Place in a roaster with water. Melt butter and stir in 3 tablespoons flour and salt; spread over chicken. Bake in a 350° oven, allowing 25 minutes per pound. (Cover with a foil tent if browning too quickly.)

Cook giblets in water to cover for 30 minutes; strain and chop.

Lift chicken from roaster when done and place on a warm platter. Remove 2 cups broth and keep warm in a saucepan for Dressing. (Recipe follows.)

For gravy, blend 2 tablespoons flour and milk. Stir into remaining broth in roaster; cook over low heat and stir until thickened. Add eggs and giblets. Add more milk if too thick.

Serves 6 to 8.

Dressing

  4 cups crumbled biscuits (made the day before)
  3 cups crumbled cornbread (made the day before)
  1 cup finely chopped onion
  ¼ cup minced parsley
  2 cups reserved chicken broth

Combine biscuits, cornbread, onion, and parsley. Add hot broth and toss lightly with a fork. Spread in a buttered baking dish, cover with foil, and bake in a 350° oven for 20 minutes. Uncover and bake an additional 10 minutes.

Double the ingredients for the holiday turkey.

Chicken and Dumplings

    1   chicken
    2   cups sifted flour
    ½   teaspoon salt
    4   level teaspoons baking powder
    1   egg
        Milk

Place chicken in a large stewpan and add water to half cover. Bring to a boil, then cover and simmer until done—1 to 2 hours.

Sift flour, salt, and baking powder. Break egg into a 1-cup measuring cup and beat lightly; then fill the cup with milk. Add to dry ingredients, beat a little, and let stand to rise for 5 minutes.

When chicken is done, remove from pan and pull meat from bones; return to simmering broth. Drop batter by spoonfuls into broth, cover, and simmer for 20 minutes.

Serves 6 to 8 in soup bowls. Just as good warmed over in broth the next day.

❧   ❧   ❧

Applejack Chicken

    1   3- to 4-pound chicken, disjointed
        Salt
    ¼   pound butter
    1   pound apples
    1   teaspoon sugar
    5   ounces applejack brandy

Sprinkle chicken with salt. Heat butter in a large frying pan and quickly sauté chicken until golden on both sides. Place in a baking dish along with butter from pan.

Peel, core, and slice apples; toss with sugar. Arrange on top of chicken. Add applejack brandy, cover, and bake in a 375° oven for about 45 minutes.

Serves 4 to 6.

Barbecued Broiler

   1   broiler chicken
   ¼   cup butter, melted
   1   cup minced onion
   2   tablespoons butter
   2   tablespoons vinegar
   2   tablespoons brown sugar
   2   tablespoons lemon juice
   1   cup catsup
   1   teaspoon salt
   2   tablespoons Worcestershire sauce
   ½   teaspoon dry mustard
   ¾   cup water
   1   clove garlic, minced
   ¼   teaspoon Tabasco sauce
   ¼   teaspoon cayenne pepper

Cut chicken in half or disjoint. Place on a broiling rack. Brush with melted butter and broil for 35 to 60 minutes, depending on the size of the chicken. Turn once.

Combine remaining ingredients in a saucepan and simmer for 20 minutes. Use to baste chicken the last 15 minutes of broiling.

Serves 2 to 4.

Buttermilk Fried Chicken

    1 2- to 3-pound fryer, cut into serving pieces
    1 teaspoon baking soda
    2 cups buttermilk
       Flour
       Cooking oil
    2 cups milk
       Salt and pepper

Wash chicken and pat dry. Dissolve soda in buttermilk. Dip chicken in buttermilk, then dredge in flour. Heat enough cooking oil to more than cover bottom of a large skillet. Cook thicker pieces of chicken first. Turn once as it browns and brown other side. When golden and done, arrange on a hot platter.

Pour off oil except for ¼ cup. Stir in 3 to 4 tablespoons flour and brown slightly, stirring up drippings to make a nice brown gravy. Slowly add milk and cook until thickened; add salt and pepper.

Serves 4 to 6.

ﾠ ﾠ ﾠ

Calico Chicken

    1 fryer
    2 tablespoons butter
    1 cup chopped onion
    1 tablespoon paprika
       Pinch cayenne pepper
       Salt and pepper
    1 cup sour cream

Cut fryer in serving pieces. Heat butter in a large skillet and simmer onion—do not brown. Remove from heat. Stir in seasonings. Lay chicken on this mixture, return to heat, cover, and simmer ¾ hour. Add a few drops of water, if necessary. Turn chicken and simmer another ¾ hour. Arrange chicken on a heated serving platter. Add sour cream to juice in pan. When heated through, pour over chicken.

Serves 4 to 6.

Company Chicken Pie

1 4- to 5-pound hen
   Pastry for 2-crust pie
6 potatoes, boiled and diced
6 hard-boiled eggs, diced
1 bell pepper, diced
2 ounces pimentos, diced
2 tablespoons flour
1 cup milk
1 heaping teaspoon salt

Boil hen in seasoned water until tender; cool. Strip meat from bones and cut in small pieces. Reserve stock and giblets for gravy.

Line a deep casserole with pastry, saving a circle for top of pie. Make layers of potatoes, eggs, bell pepper, pimentos, and chicken; repeat twice, if necessary.

Make a paste of flour and a small amount of stock in a saucepan. Slowly add 2 cups reserved stock. Cook until thickened for gravy, adding milk and salt last. Pour into casserole to within 3 inches of top—if too full it will boil over, if too little the pie will be dry. Place pastry circle on top.

Bake in a 325° oven until pie crust is brown and filling is heated through. Add diced giblets to remaining gravy and serve separately.

Serves 6 to 8.

Chicken Béarnaise

2 chicken breasts, split and boned
   Flour
3 tablespoons butter
1 teaspoon olive oil
½ cup butter
2 egg yolks
2 teaspoons lemon juice
1 teaspoon minced parsley
½ teaspoon dried tarragon
4 thick slices grilled buttered bread

Flatten chicken breasts and dredge in flour. Sizzle 3 tablespoons butter and olive oil in a frying pan; sauté chicken until golden and done. Drain.

Melt ½ cup butter in a small pan. Whisk egg yolks, lemon juice, parsley, and tarragon in a small saucepan. Place over low heat and slowly whisk in hot butter until thickened.

Place chicken breasts on grilled bread and top with sauce.
Serves 2 to 4.

ะ   ะ   ะ

Chicken à la King

2 cups diced chicken
4 tablespoons butter
1 cup chopped mushrooms
1 green pepper, shred fine
2 tablespoons flour
2 eggs, beaten
1 cup sour cream
1 pimento, diced
2 tablespoons sherry

After cooking chicken, reserve 1 cup of broth. In a large saucepan, melt butter and sauté mushrooms and green pepper. Stir in flour and blend. Slowly add chicken broth and stir until thickened. Add the chicken and cook until hot.

Combine eggs, sour cream, and pimento. Stir into chicken mixture and heat 1 to 2 minutes—do not cook. Add sherry last. Serve hot on toast, in popovers, or patty shells. Garnish with parsley.

Serves 4 to 6.

Chicken Spaghetti

2 whole chicken breasts
7 ounces thin spaghetti
¼ cup butter
½ cup flour
2 cups milk
1 cup sliced mushrooms
2 tablespoons butter
¼ cup dry white wine
1 cup shredded mozzarella cheese

Place chicken breasts in a stewpan, cover with water, and bring to a boil; reduce heat, cover pan, and simmer until done—about 1 hour. Remove chicken and when cool enough to handle, remove bones and cut up chicken. Reserve 2 cups of broth.

Boil spaghetti in water to cover until tender—about 8 minutes. Drain and rinse with hot water.

Melt ¼ cup butter in a large saucepan and blend in flour. Slowly add chicken broth and milk; stir constantly until smooth and thickened.

Sauté mushrooms in 2 tablespoons butter until soft. Add to sauce along with chicken and wine. Fold in spaghetti.

Pour into a buttered casserole and top with cheese. Bake in a 350° oven for 30 minutes until hot and bubbly.

Serves 6 to 8.

Turkey au Gratin

    4   tablespoons butter
    1   green pepper, shred fine
    1   cup sliced mushrooms
    2   tablespoons flour
    1   cup turkey broth
    1   cup milk
    1   pimento, sliced thin
    2   cups largely diced cooked turkey
    2   hard-boiled eggs, sliced
        Salt and pepper to taste
    1   ounce sherry
  ½   cup buttered breadcrumbs
  ½   cup grated cheese

Melt 2 tablespoons butter in a heavy saucepan and sauté green pepper and mushrooms; remove. Add flour to skillet and blend in remaining butter. Gradually add broth and milk; stir until thickened.

Carefully fold in pimento, turkey, eggs, salt, pepper, green pepper, and mushrooms. When heated, stir in sherry. Pour into a buttered casserole. Combine crumbs and cheese; sprinkle on top. Place under broiler until brown.

Serves 6.

Turkey Trot Hash

3 cups leftover turkey
2 tablespoons butter
2 tablespoons flour
3 cups turkey or chicken stock
1 cup finely diced cooked pototoes
1 cup diced celery
Salt and pepper to taste

Cut turkey into small pieces. Melt butter in a large saucepan and blend in flour. Slowly pour in stock and stir until thickened. Carefully stir in turkey, pototoes, and celery. Season with salt and pepper. Simmer until celery is tender.
Serves 6.

æ   æ   æ

Chicken Livers in Sour Cream

1 pound chicken livers
¼ cup butter
1 green pepper, minced
¼ pound mushrooms, sliced
2 tablespoons flour
1 pint sour cream
2 tablespoons chopped parsley
1 tablespoon grated onion
Salt and pepper to taste

Wash chicken livers and pat dry. Heat butter in a frying pan and gently sauté livers until done. Remove livers.
In same pan, sauté green pepper and mushrooms until soft. Sprinkle with flour and stir in sour cream; stir over low heat until mixture thickens. Then add parsley, onion, salt, and pepper.
Just before serving, add livers and heat thoroughly.
Serves 4 to 6.

Wild Game

Delta Duck

- 2 wild ducks
- 2 thick onion slices
- 2 thick lemon slices
  - Parsley sprigs
  - Salt
  - Flour
- ½ cup butter
- ½ cup chopped onion
- ½ cup sliced mushrooms
- 2 tablespoons minced parsley
- ½ cup white wine
- ½ cup cream

Wash ducks and pat dry. Stuff each with onion slice, lemon slice, and parsley sprigs. Roll in seasoned flour. Sizzle butter in a large frying pan and quickly brown ducks. Sprinkle in remaining seasoned flour—at least 2 tablespoons. Remove ducks and place in a large casserole.

To frying pan, add chopped onion, mushrooms and minced parsley; sauté until onions are soft. Stir in wine and pour all over ducks, adding enough water to almost cover birds. Cover and cook in a 325° oven for 3 hours or more, basting every 30 minutes.

About 10 minutes before serving, remove cover and add cream. Carve ducks, arrange on a heated platter. Serve sauce separately.

Serves 4 to 6.

ॐ　ॐ　ॐ

Roast Wild Duck

- 2 wild ducks
  - Salted water
- 1 carrot, halved
- 1 celery stalk, halved
- 2 apple wedges
- 4 slices bacon
- 4 tablespoons flour

Wash ducks and place in a pan of cold, salted water for 1 hour. Wash again and place in a small roaster. Stuff cavities with carrot, celery, and apple to absorb some of the wild taste. Crisscross two bacon slices over each breast and add 1 cup water. Cover roaster. For very rare duck, roast at 450° for 20 to 30 minutes. For well-done duck, roast at 350° for 1½ to 2 hours. Remove roaster cover during last few minutes to brown ducks.

Place ducks on a heated serving dish. Pour off all but 4 tablespoons of pan juices; reserve rest. Stir in flour and brown. Gradually add remaining pan juices and enough water (1 to 2 cups) to make gravy. Serve with Arkansas Rice Dressing (see page 137).

Serves 4 to 6, depending on size of ducks.

ᔓ   ᔓ   ᔓ.

Duck on a Stick

     4   duck breasts
  1½   cups Italian salad dressing
    ½   teaspoon garlic salt
    ¼   teaspoon lemon pepper
    ¼   cup beer
     2   onions, quartered
     1   bell pepper, cut in 1½-inch squares
     2   tomatoes, quartered (or use cherry tomatoes)
     6   mushrooms (or more)

Cut duck breasts in chunks. Place in a covered dish. Combine salad dressing, garlic salt, lemon pepper, and beer; pour over duck, cover, and marinate in refrigerator for 6 to 8 hours. Boil onions and bell pepper in water to cover until just tender. Drain, cool, and add to duck marinade, along with tomatoes and mushrooms; marinate an additional hour.

Alternate duck and vegetables on skewers. Cook on outdoor grill for 10 to 15 minutes, browning on all sides.

Serves 6.

Duck Gumbo

      4   wild ducks
      1   onion, sliced
      1   apple, peeled and chopped
    ¾   cup butter
      1   cup flour
      2   cups chopped onions
      2   cups chopped celery
    ½   cup chopped green pepper
      1   bunch green onions (tops, too), chopped
      6   ounces tomato paste
      2   16-ounce cans tomatoes, chopped
      1   teaspoon thyme
      1   teaspoon oregano
      2   bay leaves
      2   teaspoons chopped parsley
    ¼   cup sugar
      1   teaspoon black pepper
      1   teaspoon red pepper
      1   pound smoked sausage, sliced
      1   teaspoon filé powder
          Salt to taste

Boil ducks with onion and apple in water to cover until done—about 1 hour. Remove meat and cut into bite-size pieces. Strain stock and reserve. Melt butter in a large boiler and add flour to make a roux, cooking over medium heat until dark brown. Slowly stir in 2 quarts of strained duck broth. Add remaining ingredients (except sausage, filé, and salt), cover and simmer 1 hour.

Add duck meat and cook another hour, or until duck is tender. Add sausage the last 30 minutes. Add filé the last 5 minutes. Season with salt to taste. If too thick, thin with heated duck stock or water.

Serves 10 to 12. Freezes well.

Grilled Quail

Quail
Melted Butter
Salt and pepper
Thickly sliced buttered bread

Allow 1 or 2 quail per person. Split down back, brush with melted butter and season with salt and pepper. Carefully place over gray coals and cook on both sides until beautifully brown and done. Keep hot while grilling bread on both sides. Serve quail on toast with more melted butter on top.

&. &. &.

White Wine Quail

6 quail
½ cup butter
2 small onions, minced
2 whole cloves
1 teaspoon peppercorns
2 garlic cloves, minced
½ bay leaf
2 cups white wine
½ teaspoon salt
⅛ teaspoon pepper
Few grains cayenne
1 teaspoon minced chives
2 cups cream

Clean and truss quail. Melt butter in a large frying pan, add onions, cloves, peppercorns, garlic, and bay leaf; sauté until onions are limp. Add quail and brown on all sides. Add wine, salt, pepper, cayenne, and chives; cover and simmer until tender, about 30 minutes.

Remove quail to a hot serving platter. Strain remaining sauce into a saucepan, add cream, and heat to boiling. Pour over quail and serve.

Allow at least 1 quail per serving.

Quail on Toast

   2   quail
       Salt and freshly ground pepper
   1   onion
   3   apples, peeled and cored
   3   tablespoons butter
   2   tablespoons cooking oil
  ¼   cup flour
   2   cups water
  1½   cups Arkansas apple cider
       Chopped parsley
       Buttered toast

Clean quail and split down back, wipe carefully, and season with
salt and pepper. Dice onion and 1 apple; sauté in 2 tablespoons
butter and cooking oil until tender; remove and drain. Add quail
to pan and sauté until brown; remove and drain. Add flour and
cook until light brown. Stir in water, cider, onion, and apple;
simmer for 3 minutes.

   Place quail in a casserole and pour sauce on top. Cover and bake
in a 350° oven for 30 to 35 minutes. Slice remaining apples into
rings and brown lightly in remaining 1 tablespoon butter. Sprinkle
with chopped parsley. Serve quail on toast, pour sauce from casserole over birds, and garnish with apple rings and parsley.
   Serves 2.

Flyway Wild Goose

  1   6- to 8-pound wild goose
 ¼ cup dry white wine
  1   cup minced onion
  2   tablespoons butter
  2   tablespoons flour
  1   cup tomato juice
 ½ green pepper, seeded and minced
  6   ripe olives, sliced
  2   ounces sherry

Cut cleaned goose into serving pieces. Place in a heavy skillet, add dry white wine and water to cover. Cover and simmer until tender, about 1½ to 2 hours. Keep goose warm. Reserve 1 cup broth.

In a frying pan, brown minced onion in butter. Add flour and stir well. Slowly add broth and tomato juice. Stir in green pepper and olives; cook until thickened. Add sherry. Serve sauce over wild goose.

Serves 6 to 8.

Vineyard Doves

  8   doves, cleaned and dressed
     Seasoned flour
 ½ cup butter
  1   cup seedless white grapes
     Juice of 1 lemon
 ½ cup slivered blanched almonds
  8   toast squares (no crust)

Sprinkle doves with seasoned flour inside and out. Melt butter in a skillet and brown doves. Add 1 cup water, cover, and cook slowly until tender—about an hour. Do not let water evaporate, add more if necessary. Add grapes; cook about 20 minutes more. Remove birds and keep warm. Add lemon juice and almonds; simmer a few minutes. Serve doves on toast with sauce spooned on top.

Serves 8.

Dinner Party Doves

      8   doves
          Salt and pepper
      ½   cup butter
          Juice of 1½ lemons
      3   ounces sherry
      4   tablespoons Worcestershire sauce
      2   tablespoons flour
      1   cup cream

Split birds and season with salt and pepper. Melt ¼ cup butter in a large skillet and brown birds, breast down, with about 1 teaspoon of butter on each. When lightly browned, add enough water to keep birds from burning, cover, and cook 1 hour. When almost done, add lemon juice, sherry, and Worcestershire sauce. Cook another 20 minutes, then remove birds. Blend flour into cream and add to skillet; stir and let thicken for sauce. Arrange birds and sauce in a heated chafing dish.
   Serves 8.

ð   ð   ð

Rabbit Fricassee

      1   rabbit
      ½   cup flour
      1   teaspoon salt
          Pepper to taste
      1   garlic clove
      4   tablespoons cooking oil
      1   cup water

Dress and cut up rabbit; wash and drain well. Season flour with salt and pepper. Roll each piece of rabbit in flour, covering completely. Rub a frying pan with garlic and heat cooking oil; quickly brown rabbit. Arrange rabbit in a casserole. Rinse frying pan with water and pour over rabbit. Cover and bake in a 350° oven for 1½ hours.
   Serves 4.

Devil's Den Rabbit and Tomato Stew

2 rabbits
2 tablespoons butter
2 tablespoons flour
1 tablespoon minced parsley
½ teaspoon thyme
1 bay leaf
½ teaspoon allspice
1 cup chopped onion
1 9-ounce can whole tomatoes
3 cups boiling water
Salt
Cayenne pepper
Juice of 1 lemon
Parsley

Wash two dressed rabbits and cut into pieces; wipe dry. Melt butter in a stewpan and when hot, add flour, browning slowly. Stir in parsley, thyme, bay leaf, allspice, onion, and tomatoes (cut into pieces plus juice). Add boiling water and season with salt and pepper; boil 5 minutes. Then carefully add pieces of rabbit. Stir in lemon juice, cover, and simmer for 20 to 30 minutes, until rabbit is tender. Some like to simmer it for an hour or two. Garnish with parsley.

Serves 6 to 10.

Crossbow Roast Venison

1 3- to 4-pound venison roast
   Vinegar
   Flour
1 cup hot water

Rub roast with a cloth wrung out in vinegar, then dust with flour. Put in a roasting pan, adding 1 tablespoon vinegar and hot water. Cover and cook in a 325° oven for 1 hour. Uncover and cook until tender. Allow about 30 minutes per pound for total cooking time.

Remove roast to a hot platter while making gravy. Thicken pan juices with 3 tablespoons flour, adding more water if necessary. Season to taste.

Serves 10 to 12.

ঌ   ঌ   ঌ

Haunch of Venison

1 2- to 2½-pound haunch of venison
6 to 8 garlic cloves, split
   Salt and pepper
4 tablespoons butter, softened
½ cup red wine

Wash venison and dry thoroughly. With a sharp knife, make 12 to 16 gashes in venison and insert garlic. Then rub meat with salt, pepper, and butter, covering completely. Place prepared haunch in a large baking pan, add 2 cups water, and bake in a 325° oven for 2 hours. About ½ hour before venison is done, add red wine. Carve roast and serve with pan juices.

Serves 6 to 8.

Venison Pot Roast

1 3-pound venison shoulder
1 cup vinegar
1 tomato, diced
2 bay leaves
¼ teaspoon whole cloves
¼ teaspoon peppercorns
¼ cup flour
½ teaspoon pepper
1 teaspoon salt
½ teaspoon allspice
4 tablespoons butter or margarine
½ cup chopped onion
6 gingersnaps, crushed

Place roast in mixture of vinegar, tomato, bay leaves, cloves, peppercorns, and enough water to cover; refrigerate 8 to 10 hours.

Later, combine flour, pepper, salt, and allspice. Remove roast from marinade, reserving 1½ cups of the liquid. Coat roast with flour mixture. Heat butter and chopped onion in a skillet and brown roast. When brown on all sides, place in a covered casserole, add reserved marinade, and water, if necessary, to cover roast. Cover casserole and bake in a 350° oven for 2½ hours. Remove roast. Add gingersnaps to gravy, season to taste and serve.

Serves 6 to 8.

Venison Sausage

½ pound finely chopped raw venison
½ pound finely chopped salt pork
3 teaspoons sage
1½ teaspoons salt
1 teaspoon pepper

Thoroughly combine all ingredients. Form into 8 flat cakes and fry with no other fat, as that in the sausage is sufficient. Fry until golden brown and done through. Drain.

Serves 4 to 8.

ð. ð. ð.

Fried Squirrel

2 young squirrels
½ cup milk
1 teaspoon salt
½ teaspoon pepper
½ cup flour
4 tablespoons cooking oil
2 tablespoons butter
2 tablespoons flour
   Milk

Cut squirrels into serving pieces. Dip in milk and coat with seasoned flour. Heat oil and butter in a skillet and brown pieces of squirrel on all sides over high heat; reduce temperature, cover skillet, and cook until done—about 45 minutes. Remove cover last few minutes for crispness.

Drain squirrel on absorbent paper. Pour off all but 2 tablespoons of oil in pan, stir in 2 tablespoons flour and enough milk to thicken for gravy.

Serves 4 to 6.

If you fry the heads for the brains, remember to bring a hammer to the table.

Hunter's Brunswick Stew

2 squirrels
3 slices bacon
1 onion, sliced thin
1 gallon water
1 quart tomatoes, peeled
2 ears corn, grated
3 Irish potatoes, peeled and cubed
½ pint shelled butter beans
½ pod red pepper, chopped
1 tablespoon bread crumbs
1 tablespoon butter
   Salt and pepper

Prepare squirrels for cooking. Combine squirrels, bacon, and onion with water in a large stewpan. Bring to a boil and simmer until meat is tender. Remove squirrels and pull meat from bones and skin. Cut up meat and return to broth. Add tomatoes, corn, potatoes, butter beans, and pepper. Cook until all vegetables are tender, 1 to 2 hours. Stir in bread crumbs and butter. Season with salt and pepper.

Serves 8 to 10.

Barbecue Sauce for Wild Game

2 tablespoons honey
4 tablespoons butter
1 cup catsup
3 tablespoons Worcestershire sauce
   Juice of ½ lemon
1 teaspoon onion salt
1 teaspoon garlic salt
1 tablespoon prepared mustard

Mix all ingredients in a saucepan and cook slowly for about 15 minutes.

Lay game on foil paper, spooning the sauce generously on top. Wrap the foil around the meat, securing edges tightly so that sauce cannot run out. Cook in a 350° oven for 2 to 3 hours, or until game is tender.

Vegetables

Potluck Dinner Asparagus

2 8½-ounce cans asparagus tips
2 tablespoons butter
2 tablespoons flour
1 cup milk
3 hard-boiled eggs, sliced
1 cup grated cheese

Drain asparagus and reserve juice. Melt butter in a saucepan and stir in flour. Gradually add milk and reserved juice; stir until thickened.

Arrange asparagus and eggs in a casserole. Pour over sauce; sprinkle with grated cheese. Bake in a 350° oven for about 25 minutes.

Serves 6 to 8.

ða ða ða

Log Cabin Baked Beans

2 cups dried pea beans
½ pound salt pork, diced
1 medium-sized onion, chopped
2 tablespoons brown sugar
4 tablespoons molasses
1 cup chili sauce
   Salt and pepper
4 slices bacon

Soak beans overnight in cold water to cover. In the morning, add enough water to cover, stir in salt pork, and simmer about 1 hour or until beans are tender. Drain and reserve liquid.

Layer beans and onion in a bean pot or casserole. Combine brown sugar, molasses, chili sauce, salt, pepper, and 1 cup reserved liquid; pour over top of beans. Place bacon slices on top and bake until beans are thick—2 hours or longer—in a 300° oven.

Serves 4 to 6.

Sweet and Sour Green Beans

    6   cups cooked green beans
    4   slices bacon
    ½   cup water
    1   tablespoon sugar
    ½   teaspoon salt
    ⅓   cup vinegar
    1   onion, sliced thin

Drain green beans. Fry bacon until crisp; drain. To drippings left in pan, add water, sugar, salt, vinegar, and onion. Stir in green beans and simmer 15 minutes. Crumble bacon on top when serving.
    Serves 8 to 10.

Fried Cabbage

    1   pound cabbage
    ¼   cup shortening or bacon drippings
    ½   teaspoon salt
        Dash pepper
    ½   teaspoon sugar
    ¼   cup water

Shred cabbage. Heat shortening or bacon drippings in a skillet and stir in cabbage; sprinkle with seasonings. Add water, cover, and simmer 7 to 10 minutes. Serve immediately.
    Serves 4.

Baked Carrots

1   cup hot mashed carrots
1   egg, beaten
1   teaspoon salt
1   tablespoon sugar
½   teaspoon pepper
⅓   cup grated cheese
6   tablespoons melted butter
1½ cups milk
½   cup cracker crumbs

Combine carrots with egg, salt, sugar, pepper, cheese, and 4 tablespoons melted butter. Alternately add milk and ¼ cup cracker crumbs. Place in a buttered baking dish and bake at 350° for about 30 minutes. Toss remaining ¼ cup cracker crumbs and 2 tablespoons butter; sprinkle on top of carrots. Return to oven and brown.
    Serves 2 to 4.

≈   ≈   ≈

Old-Time Corn Pudding

2   cups cream-style yellow corn
2   tablespoons butter, softened
1   tablespoon minced onion
½   cup minced green pepper
1   pimento, minced
3   eggs
2   cups milk
2   tablespoons sugar
1   teaspoon salt

Combine corn with butter, onion, green pepper, and pimento. Beat eggs slightly; stir in milk, sugar, and salt. Combine mixtures and blend. Turn into a buttered casserole and bake at 325° for 1 hour.
    Serves 6 to 8.

Fried Corn

3½ cups corn
½ cup diced bacon
1 teaspoon sugar
1 teaspoon salt
⅛ teaspoon pepper
¾ cup milk

If fresh corn is not available, frozen will do (thaw first). Fry bacon until crisp and drain off all but 3 tablespoons of drippings. Stir in corn, sugar, salt, and pepper; cook about 12 minutes, or until lightly browned, stirring often. Add milk and continue cooking until milk disappears. Then cook another 5 to 10 minutes.

Serves 6 to 8.

ە ە ە

Corn Fritters

2 cups corn
1⅓ cups flour
1 teaspoon salt
1½ teaspoons baking powder
⅔ cup milk
1 egg, beaten

Freshly cut corn from cobs is best. Sift flour, salt, and baking powder. Combine milk and egg; beat thoroughly. Add to dry ingredients; mix until flour is moistened. Then stir in corn. Drop by tablespoons into hot cooking oil (365° to 375°). Fry until golden brown. Serve immediately.

Makes about 1½ dozen.

Eggplant Casserole

1 medium-sized eggplant
1 medium-sized onion, chopped
½ teaspoon salt
1 cup grated cheese
1 egg, beaten
Dash red pepper
½ cup crushed crackers
4 tablespoons butter

Peel and quarter eggplant. Combine eggplant, onion, and salt in a saucepan. Cook in a small amount of water about 15 minutes, until vegetables are tender. Drain and mash. Blend in cheese, egg, and pepper. Pour into a buttered casserole and cover with crackers. Dot with butter. Bake in a 350° oven for 30 minutes.

Serves 4 to 8.

❧   ❧   ❧

Fried Eggplant

1 eggplant
1 egg, beaten
1 tablespoon flour
1 tablespoon sugar
Cooking oil

Peel eggplant and slice. Put in a saucepan with water to cover and bring to a boil; cover saucepan and simmer until eggplant is tender. Drain eggplant and mash. Blend in egg, flour, and sugar.

Heat cooking oil in a skillet and drop spoonfuls of batter into hot oil. Fry until golden on both sides, turning only once.

Serves 2 to 4.

Wild Greens

Pick a mess of greens in the early morning while they are moist with dew. Look for Lamb's Quarter, Dandelions, Old Hen and Chicken, Plantain, Hen Pepper, Narrow Leaf Dock, Mouse Ears, Speckled Breeches, Old Sate, Wild Lettuce, Greenbrier Sprouts, Poke, Wild Mustard, and Watercress.

1   pound wild greens
1   small ham hock or pieces of ham

Pick through greens to remove any discolored leaves. Place in a colander and run under cold water to strain any soil. Arrange ham and greens in a large stewpan; cover with water. Bring to a boil, cover, and simmer until greens are tender. Occasionally turn greens with a fork.
 Serves 4.

&a   &a   &a

Fried Mushrooms

Fresh mushrooms
Salted water
Flour or cornmeal

Wash and clean mushrooms with a soft brush. Soak in salted water for several hours; drain. Dredge in flour or cornmeal to coat. Pan-fry like chicken or fish in cooking oil. Serve piping hot!

Hoppingjohn

Always serve on New Year's Day. This is enough to serve a crowd when only a taste will bring good luck!

½ pound slab smoked bacon, sliced thin
1 cup black-eyed peas
½ cup diced onion
3 cups water
½ cup rice

Fry bacon, drain, and reserve drippings. Combine peas, onion, and bacon drippings with water in a saucepan. Bring to a boil and then simmer until tender—about 1 hour.

Cook rice until fluffy. Stir into peas. Add bacon and simmer a few more minutes.

> ❧ ❧ ❧

Horseshoe Bend Squash

6 crookneck squash
1 cup bread crumbs
2 tablespoons melted butter
1 egg, beaten
1 tablespoon minced onion
1 tablespoon minced parsley
1 teaspoon salt
¼ teaspoon white pepper

Parboil squash until just tender; drain. Halve squash and scoop out pulp, leaving stems intact.

Toss bread crumbs with melted butter, reserving 2 tablespoons for toppings. Mix hot squash pulp with buttered crumbs and stir in remaining ingredients. Spoon into squash shells. Sprinkle with reserved crumbs. Bake in a 350° oven until tops are puffy and delicately brown.

Serves 10 to 12.

Brandied Sweet Potatoes

2½ pounds sweet potatoes
¼ pound margarine or butter
½ cup light brown sugar
1 teaspoon cinnamon
¼ teaspoon nutmeg
½ teaspoon salt
½ cup brandy

Boil sweet potatoes in skins until soft. Remove from water and cool. Peel and cut into 1½-inch slices. Place in 1 layer in a buttered shallow baking dish. Dot with margarine or butter. Mix brown sugar, cinnamon, nutmeg, and salt; sprinkle over potatoes. Pour brandy over all. Bake in a 375° oven for 30 minutes.

Serves 6 to 8.

Yam Surprise

3 cups hot mashed sweet potatoes
½ cup brown sugar
½ cup butter, softened
½ cup cream
¼ teaspoon cinnamon
¼ teaspoon nutmeg
¾ cup diced marshmallows

Thoroughly combine all ingredients except marshmallows. Spoon into a buttered casserole and top with marshmallows. Bake in a 350° oven until golden brown.

Serves 6 to 8.

Puffy Turnips

    2   cups hot mashed turnips
    1½   cups hot mashed potatoes
    3   tablespoons melted butter
    1   egg, beaten
    ½   teaspoon salt
    ⅛   teaspoon white pepper
    2 to 3 tablespoons cream

Combine turnips and potatoes. Lightly stir in remaining ingredients. Mound in a buttered baking dish and bake at 375° for 25 minutes.

Serves 6 to 8.

Sweets

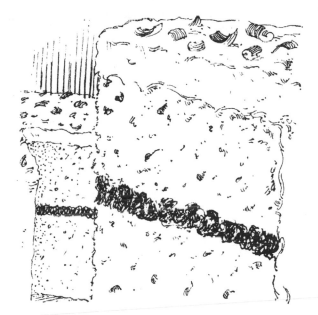

Ambrosia

An Arkansas Christmas favorite

> 3 large Valencia oranges (usually available during
> the holidays)
> ½ cup (or more) powdered sugar
> 1½ cups shredded coconut (fresh is best)

Peel oranges and remove all white membrane while separating into sections; thinly slice, if possible.

Alternate layers of oranges, powdered sugar, and coconut in a decorative serving bowl. Top with powdered sugar and coconut to cover top. Cover and chill well.

Serves 4 to 5.

ða   ða   ða

Charlotte Russe

> 1 pint cream, whipped
> 2 egg whites, beaten until stiff
> 1 cup (scant) powdered sugar, sifted
> ½ ounce gelatin
> ½ cup hot milk
> ½ teaspoon vanilla
> 2 drops almond extract
> Lady fingers

Carefully fold and blend cream, egg whites, and sugar; chill. Dissolve gelatin in hot milk; cool. Stir into chilled mixture, adding vanilla and almond extract.

Line a glass bowl with lady fingers and fill with custard mixture. Chill in refrigerator for a least 4 hours before serving.

Serves 6 to 8.

Rum Torte

2 tablespoons gelatin
1 cup cold water
12 almond macaroons
¼ cup rum
2 cups milk
4 eggs, separated
¾ cup sugar
4 tablespoons sugar
1 teaspoon vanilla
1 tablespoon rum

Soak gelatin in cold water. Soften macaroons in ¼ cup rum. Scald milk in a heavy saucepan—heat until bubbles appear at edges of pan. Beat egg yolks and add to milk, along with ¾ cup sugar; cook until thickened. Add gelatin and dissolve. Remove from heat and cool until mixture begins to thicken.

Beat egg whites until stiff, gradually adding 4 tablespoons sugar, vanilla, and 1 tablespoon rum. Fold into cooled custard.

Line a springform pan with macaroons. Carefully pour custard mixture into pan and chill for at least 8 hours.

Unmold and garnish with whipped cream, if desired.
Serves 6 to 10.

&a.   &a.   &a.

Ruth Malone's Pound Cake

¾ pound butter, softened
1 16-ounce box powdered sugar
6 eggs
  Cake flour (measure after sifting same amount as
    powdered sugar—measure in powdered sugar box)
1 teaspoon mace or ½ teaspoon lemon extract

In large electric mixer bowl, cream butter and gradually add sugar. Add eggs, one at a time; then flour. Flavor with mace or lemon extract.

Bake in an ungreased tube or bundt pan for 1 hour at 350°.

Chocolate Cream Roll

  6   eggs, separated
  ¾   cup sugar
  ½   cup (scant) cocoa
  ¼   cup flour
  ½   teaspoon salt
  1   teaspoon baking powder
  1   teaspoon vanilla
      Sifted powdered sugar

Beat egg yolks until thick; gradually add ¼ cup sugar and beat until lemon colored. Sift cocoa, flour, salt, and baking powder; blend into first mixture. Beat egg whites until stiff, gradually adding remaining ½ cup sugar; fold into batter. Flavor with vanilla.

Line a jellyroll pan with waxed paper and spread batter evenly. Bake in a 375° oven for 12 minutes. Turn out on a fresh tea towel covered with sifted powdered sugar. Roll cake with tea towel; cool. Unroll and spread with Whipped Cream Filling (recipe follows), reserving a little to decorate top.

Serves 8.

Whipped Cream Filling

  1   pint cream
  ¼   cup sifted powdered sugar
      Dash sherry or vanilla

Whip cream until stiff, gradually adding powdered sugar and flavoring.

Southern White Christmas Fruit Cake

- 1 cup butter, softened
- 2 cups sugar
- 3 cups flour, before sifting
- ¾ pound candied cherries
- ¾ pound candied pineapple
- ½ pound candied citron
- 1 pound pecans, coarsely chopped
- 1 teaspoon baking powder
- 12 egg whites
- 1 teaspoon vanilla
- 1 ounce bourbon (optional)

Cream butter and sugar; gradually work in 1½ cups flour. Coarsely chop fruit, reserving some to decorate top of cake. Stir in ½ of fruits and nuts into butter mixture.

Sift baking powder with remaining flour; stir in remaining fruit and nuts. Beat egg whites until stiff and gently fold in to blend. Combine mixtures. Stir in vanilla and bourbon.

Pour batter into a greased tube pan lined with waxed paper. Bake at 275° for 2½ hours. After cake has baked about 1 hour decorate top with reserved fruit. Immediately return to oven until cake is done.

Wondering what to do with so many egg yolks? Try Pot O'Gold Cake (page 118).

Fudge Cake

½ cup butter, softened
2 cups sugar
2 eggs
1 teaspoon baking soda
2 cups flour
3 tablespoons cocoa
½ cup buttermilk
1 cup boiling water

Cream butter and sugar. Beat in eggs, one at a time. Sift soda, flour, and cocoa; add alternately with buttermilk. Stir in boiling water. (This is a very thin batter.) Pour in a greased 10 x 14-inch pan. Bake at 350° for 30 to 35 minutes.

Spread Chocolate Fudge Icing (recipe follows) on top of cake and cut into squares.

Chocolate Fudge Icing

3 cups sugar
3 tablespoons cocoa
1 cup cream
¼ cup butter
¼ teaspoon salt
1 teaspoon vanilla

Combine ingredients in a saucepan and cook until soft ball stage (234° - 238°). Cool and beat until thickened.

Strawberry Jam Cake

    ¾ cup butter, softened
    1 cup sugar
    3 eggs, separated
    1 teaspoon baking soda
    2 teaspoons milk
  2½ cups flour
    1 teaspoon nutmeg
    1 teaspoon allspice
    1 teaspoon cinnamon
    1 cup strawberry jam
    3 tablespoons buttermilk

Cream butter and sugar. Beat egg yolks and blend into butter and sugar. Dissolve soda in milk; add to first mixture. Sift flour and spices. Add alternately to batter with jam and buttermilk. Beat egg whites and fold in last. Fill 2 greased layer cake pans and bake at 350° for 30 minutes. Cool.

Spread Burnt Caramel Icing (recipe follows) between layers, on top, and on sides of cake.

Burnt Caramel Icing

    3 cups sugar
    1 cup milk

Combine 2 cups sugar and milk in a heavy saucepan; let come to a boil. Heat 1 cup sugar in an iron skillet and stir until beautifully brown. Slowly add to boiling mixture; cook about 10 minutes. Remove from heat and beat until spreadable.

Pumpkin Cake

¾ cup cooked pumpkin
½ cup butter, softened
1 cup brown sugar
½ cup sugar
2 eggs, separated
2 cups flour
1 teaspoon baking powder
¼ teaspoon baking soda
1 teaspoon salt
1 teaspoon cinnamon
⅓ cup sour cream or cream
⅔ cup chopped nuts

Mash pumpkin. Cream butter and sugars. Beat egg yolks and stir in along with pumpkin. Sift flour, baking powder, soda, salt, and cinnamon. Stir into creamed mixture alternately with sour cream or cream. Beat egg whites until stiff and fold in gently. Stir in nuts. Pour into two 8-inch cake pans lined with waxed paper. Bake at 350° for 25 minutes; cool.

Spread Spiced Whipped Cream (recipe follows) between layers.

Spiced Whipped Cream

1 cup cream
3 tablespoons powdered sugar
1 teaspoon cinnamon
1 teaspoon ginger

Whip cream, gradually adding powdered sugar, cinnamon, and ginger. Chill.

Pioneer Wedding Stack Cake

This was a favorite wedding cake in the early days when sugar was not plentiful. Wedding guests brought a thin layer of sorghum cake to add to the bride's cake. A bride took great pride in the height of her cake—a higher cake denoted more friends. Some say the footed cake stand became popular for this reason. The bride's mother furnished applesauce to go between layers. Stack layers are similar to a rich cookie dough.

1½   cups sifted flour
½   teaspoon baking powder
½   teaspoon salt
½   teaspoon baking soda
½   cup sugar
½   cup shortening
1   egg, beaten
½   cup sorghum
1   tablespoon milk
1   teaspoon vanilla

Sift together flour, baking powder, salt, soda, and sugar. Cut in shortening until mixture looks like coarse meal. Blend in egg, sorghum, milk, and vanilla.

Divide dough into 3 parts. Roll out on a floured board and cut the size of a dinner plate. Bake on an ungreased cookie sheet at 375° for about 8 minutes.

Spread applesauce or frosting between stacks.

Pot O'Gold Cake

½ cup butter, softened
1½ cups sugar
10 egg yolks, well beaten
1 teaspoon vanilla or lemon extract
2½ cups flour
2 teaspoons baking powder
1 cup milk

Cream butter and sugar. Combine with egg yolks; beat again. Add flavoring. Sift flour and baking powder. Add alternately with milk to first mixture. Beat well.

Pour batter into a buttered tube or loaf pan. Bake at 325° for 40 minutes.

ઙ ઙ ઙ

Sorghum Gingerbread

½ cup butter, softened
½ cup sugar
1 egg, beaten
1 cup sorghum (or molasses)
2½ cups sifted flour
1 teaspoon baking soda
1 teaspoon cinnamon
½ teaspoon ground cloves
1 teaspoon ginger
½ teaspoon salt
1 cup hot water

Cream butter and sugar. Stir in egg and sorghum. Sift dry ingredients; blend into batter. Then stir in hot water. (The batter is soft, but makes a fine cake.)

Pour into a greased shallow pan. Bake in a 350° oven for 30 to 35 minutes.

Fudge Frosted Brownies

  2 1-ounce squares unsweetened chocolate
  1 cup sugar
  ½ cup butter, softened
  2 eggs
  1 teaspoon vanilla
  ½ cup flour
  ½ cup chopped nuts (optional)

Melt chocolate. Cream sugar and butter; add eggs and beat. Blend in melted chocolate and vanilla. Stir in flour, adding nuts, if desired. Pour batter into a buttered 8 x 8 x 2-inch pan. Bake in a 325° oven for 35 minutes. When done, lightly press around edges of pan with the bottom of a glass to level top.

Cool before spreading with Fudge Frosting (recipe follows).

Fudge Frosting

  1 cup sifted powdered sugar
  1 tablespoon cocoa
  2 tablespoons cream
  1 tablespoon butter

Cook sugar, cocoa, cream, and butter in a saucepan until mixture boils around the sides of pan. Remove from heat and beat until thick and spreadable.

Heirloom Hermits

  1   cup butter, softened
1½ cups sugar
  3   eggs, beaten
3½ cups flour
  3   tablespoons cinnamon
 ½ teaspoon baking soda
2½ tablespoons boiling water
  1   cup chopped nuts
  1   cup raisins

Cream butter, adding sugar and eggs. Sift flour with cinnamon. Dissolve soda in boiling water; add alternately with spiced flour to butter mixture. Stir in nuts and raisins. Drop by spoonfuls onto a cookie sheet about 1 inch apart. Bake in a 350° oven for 15 to 18 minutes, or until brown.

Makes 3 to 4 dozen.

᪐   ᪐   ᪐

Lunchbox Pecan Sticks

 ¼ cup butter, softened
 1 cup brown sugar
 1 egg, beaten
 1 teaspoon vanilla
 ¼ teaspoon salt
 1 cup chopped pecans
 1 cup flour
 1 teaspoon baking powder

Cream butter and sugar. Stir in egg, vanilla, salt, and pecans. Sift flour with baking powder; combine with first mixture. Spread evenly in a buttered 8 x 8-inch pan. Bake in a 350° oven for 30 minutes. Cut when cool.

Makes about 16 pecan sticks.

Oatmeal Cookies

¾ cup shortening
1 cup sugar
2 eggs
2 cups flour
3 tablespoons cinnamon
1½ teaspoons baking powder
Pinch salt
¾ cup milk
1 cup raisins
1 cup chopped nuts
2 cups dry oatmeal

Cream shortening, gradually adding sugar and eggs. Sift flour, cinnamon, baking powder, and salt together; add to batter alternately with milk. Stir in raisins, chopped nuts, and oatmeal.

Drop by spoonfuls onto a greased baking sheet. Sprinkle with sugar and bake in a 350° oven for 10 to 12 minutes.

Makes about 2 dozen cookies.

🐚 🐚 🐚

Foolproof Pastry

2¼ cups sifted flour
1 teaspoon salt
¼ cup water
¾ cup shortening

Blend flour and salt in a bowl. Measure out ⅓ cup and make a paste with the water. Cut shortening into the rest of the flour and salt mixture until it is the size of coarse crumbs. Combine the two mixtures and stir with a pastry fork until dough comes together and can be made into a ball. Divide into 2 parts. Roll out both crusts about ⅛ inch thick on a floured board.

This amount is for a double 9-inch pie or 2 bottom crusts. If recipe calls for a baked pie crust, prick crust and bake in a 425° oven for 8 to 10 minutes.

Antebellum Chess Pie

½ cup butter
1½ cups sugar
3 eggs, separated
2 tablespoons flour
½ cup milk
1 teaspoon vanilla
1 unbaked pie crust
½ cup sugar
⅛ teaspoon cream of tartar

Cream butter, 1½ cups sugar, egg yolks, and flour. Add milk and vanilla; beat until smooth. Pour into pie crust and bake in a 325° oven for 45 to 50 minutes, until filling is set.

Beat egg whites, gradually adding ½ cup sugar and cream of tartar. When glossy and holding peaks, pile on pie. Bake at 325° for 10 to 15 minutes or until lightly browned.

❧   ❧   ❧

Huckleberry Pie

2½ cups huckleberries
1½ cups sugar
3 tablespoons cornstarch
Pinch salt
1 tablespoon lemon juice
2 tablespoons melted butter
Pastry for 2-crust pie

Wash berries and sprinkle with sugar and cornstarch. Add salt and stir until blended. Toss in lemon juice and let stand for a few minutes. Blend in butter.

Pour into bottom crust. Cover with top crust; crimp and prick. Sprinkle additional melted butter and sugar on top, if desired. Bake in a 450° oven for 10 minutes; reduce temperature to 350° and bake an additional 30 to 35 minutes, or until crust is brown.

Jam Pie

      2   eggs, separated
      ½   cup sugar
      ½   cup jam (homemade is best)
      ½   cup cream
      ½   tablespoon butter, softened
     1½   teaspoons flour
      ⅛   teaspoon nutmeg
      ⅛   teaspoon allspice
      1   unbaked pie crust
      ¼   teaspoon cream of tartar
      ¼   cup sugar

Beat egg yolks with ½ cup sugar, jam, cream, butter, flour, nutmeg, and allspice. Pour into pie shell. Bake at 300° for 45 to 60 minutes.

    Beat egg whites until they stand in peaks. Gradually add cream of tartar and ¼ cup sugar. Pile on top of pie and bake about 15 minutes at 375°.

                        ❧   ❧   ❧

Black Walnut Pie

      ½   cup black walnuts (or pecans)
      2   cups light brown sugar
      2   eggs, beaten
      ½   cup cream
      ½   teaspoon vanilla
      2   tablespoons butter, softened
      1   unbaked pie crust

Chop nuts. Blend brown sugar, eggs, cream, vanilla, and butter. Fold in nuts. Pour into pie shell. Bake at 400° for 5 to 10 minutes; reduce heat to 325° and continue baking until pie is firm—about 40 minutes.

Irish Butter Tarts

Pastry for 1-crust pie
½ cup butter, softened
1 cup sugar
2 eggs
1 cup currants

Line miniature muffin tins with pastry. Cream butter and sugar together until smooth. Add eggs and beat. Stir in currants. Fill shells and bake in a 400° oven for 25 minutes, or until tops of tarts are brown.

Makes 12 tarts.

ᔑ ᔑ ᔑ

Fresh Peach Cobbler

3 cups fresh ripe peaches, peeled, pitted, and sliced
2 tablespoons lemon juice
1 cup sugar
2 tablespoons flour
Pastry for 2-crust pie
1 egg white
4 tablespoons butter
½ cup water (or more)

Sprinkle peaches with lemon juice to prevent darkening. Toss peaches with ½ cup sugar and flour.

Roll out pastry into 1 large oblong piece. Line an oblong baking dish with pastry, leaving enough to fold over and across the top. Brush bottom of pastry with egg white. Spread peaches on pastry, sprinkle with remaining sugar, and dot with butter. Add water. Fold pastry over to cover; crimp. Sprinkle additional sugar on top, if desired.

Bake in a 425° oven for 35 to 40 minutes, or until pastry is golden.

Serves 6 to 8.

Strawberry Shortcake

1   pint strawberries
¼   cup powdered sugar
    Pastry for 2-crust pie

Wash and hull strawberries, reserving a few for decoration. Mash berries with sugar. Chill at least 30 minutes so sugar will dissolve in juice.

Roll out pastry and cut into 12 circles about the size of a coffee cup. Place on a cookie sheet, prick, and bake at 450° for a few minutes until golden. Watch carefully as they burn easily.

Place 6 circles on serving plates. Spoon strained strawberries on top. Cap with another pastry circle and drizzle with sweetened strawberry juice. Decorate with whole berries.

Serves 6.

&a   &a   &a

Apple Country Pudding

1   cup peeled, cored, and chopped Arkansas apples
1   teaspoon lemon juice
1   egg
⅔   cup sugar
¼   cup sifted flour
¼   teaspoon salt
1½   teaspoons baking powder
½   cup chopped nuts (preferably black walnuts)

Sprinkle apples with lemon juice. Beat egg until thick and lemon colored; gradually add sugar, flour, salt, and baking powder. Fold in apples and nuts. Pour into a buttered baking dish and bake at 350° for 30 minutes, or until crisp. The pudding will rise, then fall a little.

Serve with whipped cream.

Country-Style Rice Pudding

¼ cup butter, softened
½ cup sugar
2 eggs, separated
1 cup cooked rice
½ teaspoon cornstarch
½ cup raisins
½ cup milk
½ cup jelly (optional)

Cream butter and ½ cup sugar. Beat egg yolks until light; stir in rice and cornstarch. Combine with first mixture. Stir in raisins and milk. Pour into a buttered baking dish. Bake in a 350° oven until brown on top and soft underneath—about 30 minutes.

If desired, beat jelly and spread over hot pudding. Beat egg whites until stiff and gradually add 2 tablespoons sugar; pile on pudding. Bake in a 325° oven for 10 to 15 minutes until delicately brown.

Serves 4.

❧   ❧   ❧

Sweet Potato Pudding

2 cups grated sweet potatoes
½ teaspoon cinnamon
½ teaspoon nutmeg
½ cup butter, softened
1 cup sugar
2 eggs
1 cup milk
½ pint cream

Toss sweet potatoes with cinnamon and nutmeg. Cream butter and sugar; beat in eggs. Combine with sweet potatoes and stir in milk. Pour into a buttered baking dish and sprinkle with additional cinnamon and nutmeg. Bake at 375° for 20 minutes.

Serve with cream or whipped cream on top.

Persimmon Pudding

Wait until after the first frost before gathering or buying persimmons.

    1   quart ripe persimmons
    2   cups milk
    1   cup butter, softened
 1½   cups sugar
    1   teaspoon ground cloves
    1   teaspoon cinnamon
    1   teaspoon nutmeg
    3   eggs, well beaten
    3   cups flour
    ¼   teaspoon ginger
    ¼   teaspoon allspice

Wash and rub persimmons through a colander; stir in milk. Cream butter and sugar; blend in cloves, cinnamon, and nutmeg. Stir in persimmon mixture and eggs. Sift flour with ginger and allspice. Combine all and pour into a buttered baking dish. Bake in a 300° oven for 1½ to 2 hours.

ra   ra   ra

Walnut Brittle

    2   cups sugar
 1½   cups coarsely chopped black walnuts
         Pinch salt

Melt sugar in a heavy iron skillet over low heat, stirring constantly so sugar will not scorch. When it becomes a thin golden syrup, remove from heat. Stir in walnuts and salt. Spread on an ungreased tin or marble slab to harden.

Mark into squares when nearly cold or break into irregular pieces when hardened.

Bachelor Buttons

2¼ cups brown sugar
½ cup thin cream
2 tablespoons butter
1 cup pecans

Combine brown sugar, cream, butter, and pecans in a heavy saucepan. Stir over moderate heat and let come to a boil—do not stir after it boils. Boil until a soft ball forms in cold water (236° on candy thermometer). Remove from heat and let cool. When cool, beat until smooth and thick. Drop by small spoonfuls onto waxed paper.
Makes about 30.

❧   ❧   ❧

Divinity Puffs

1½ cups sugar
2 tablespoons light corn syrup
¼ cup water
1 egg white, beaten stiff
1 drop peppermint extract (optional)

Combine sugar, syrup, and water in a heavy saucepan. Heat and stir until sugar dissolves. Cook until a soft ball stage (234° to 238°). Slowly pour syrup over egg white, beating until mixture holds shape when dropped from a spoon. Stir in peppermint extract, if desired. Drop onto waxed paper to harden.
Makes about 20.

Vinegar Taffy

    2   tablespoons butter
    4   cups sugar
    ⅔   cup boiling water
    ¼   cup mild vinegar
    1   teaspoon vanilla

Melt butter in a heavy saucepan. Add sugar, boiling water, and vinegar; stir until sugar dissolves. Cover and boil 3 minutes. Remove cover, add vanilla and continue boiling until candy thermometer registers 264° (brittle when tested in cold water).

Turn onto a buttered platter or marble slab. When cool enough to handle, butter fingers and pull taffy until porous and white. Let harden in strips. Break into pieces when cold.

ಜ   ಜ   ಜ

Peach Ice Cream

    6   cups fresh ripe peaches (peeled, pitted, and mashed)
        Juice of 6 lemons
    4   cups sugar
    1   pint cream
    2   quarts milk

Mix peaches, lemon juice, and sugar; let stand 30 minutes. Quickly stir in cream and milk. Fill ice cream freezer container ¾ full. Freeze until hard. Remove dasher and cover until serving time.

Makes approximately 2½ to 3 quarts.

Spreads

Grape Arbor Jelly

1½ pounds Arkansas grapes
1½ pounds sugar

Put grapes in a heavy saucepan and sprinkle sugar on top. Bring to a boil and simmer 25 minutes. Strain through a sieve or cheesecloth. Pour into sterilized jars and seal.
    Makes about 2½ pints.

ਡ਼   ਡ਼   ਡ਼

Honey Butter

This is especially delicious on hot biscuits.

½ cup butter, softened
½ cup honey

Beat butter at high speed of electric mixer until creamy. Gradually add honey and beat until blended. Pour into a covered container and refrigerate.
    Makes 1 cup.

ਡ਼   ਡ਼   ਡ਼

Quick Peach Preserves

9 cups firm peaches, peeled, pitted, and sliced
¾ cup water
6 cups sugar

Boil peaches in water until just tender, stirring frequently. Strain peaches out and reserve. Add sugar to the juices and boil until mixture spins a thread (233°). Return peaches to pan and cook rapidly for 15 minutes. Pour in sterilized jars and seal.
    Makes about 2 pints.

Persimmon Spread

1 quart ripe persimmon pulp
½ cup orange juice
3 cups sugar

Cook ripe persimmon pulp in a double boiler until soft. Add orange juice and cook until thick. Stir in sugar and simmer until sugar is dissolved and mixture is thick. Pour into sterilized jars and seal.

Makes about 2 pints.

આ   આ   આ

Simple Strawberry Preserves

4 cups whole strawberries
1 cup water
4 cups sugar

Wash strawberries and drain. Blend water and 2 cups sugar in a large saucepan; boil until crystallized (230° - 234°), or will spin a thread. Then stir in 2 cups strawberries and cook for 10 minutes.

Add remaining strawberries and sugar; boil an additional 10 minutes. Pour into either a large enamel or glass container and leave at room temperature for 48 hours. Stir the berries as often as possible during the cooling period.

Pour into sterilized jars and seal. Shake often. Each time the berries are shaken they absorb more juice and become plumper.

Makes 3 to 4 cups.

Natural Wonders

⁂

Eggplant Bonfire

This is hands-on fun for everyone—whether your guests are a Brownie Troop or a sophisticated cocktail group.

  1 large eggplant
  1 can sterno heat
     Cocktail-size wieners or sausage
     Cocktail toothpicks

Cut top from eggplant and scoop out only enough pulp for sterno can to fit snugly inside. Shave bottom of eggplant so it will stand firmly on end. Place sterno can in eggplant and arrange on a wooden tray decorated with parsley.

At serving time, light sterno and let guests cook their own wieners or sausages on toothpicks over the fire.

Purple cabbage may be substituted for eggplant.

❧ ❧ ❧

Cheddar Cheese Straws

  2 cups grated sharp Cheddar cheese
  ½ cup butter, melted
1½ teaspoons salt
  ½ teaspoon red pepper
  2 cups sifted flour

Blend all ingredients until a dough forms. Roll out on a lightly floured board until thin; cut in narrow strips about 5 inches long. Bake on a cookie sheet at 400° until golden—about 6 to 8 minutes.

If preferred, shape into a log, cover with waxed paper and refrigerate. Then cut in thin slices and bake.

Arkansas Rice Dressing

4 cups cooked Arkansas rice
1 tablespoon cooking oil
1 tablespoon flour
2 cups duck or chicken broth
1 tablespoon chopped duck or chicken giblets (cooked)
1 cup chopped onion
2 tablespoons chopped parsley

While cooking rice, heat cooking oil and flour in a large saucepan; sauté until brown. Slowly add broth and stir until smooth. Add giblets, onion, and parsley; simmer for 20 minutes. Mix in cooked rice and heat.

Serves 8 to 10.

❧   ❧   ❧

Vineyard Grape Catsup

4 pounds seedless red grapes
3 pounds sugar
1 teaspoon allspice
1 teaspoon salt
2 teaspoons cinnamon
1 cup tarragon vinegar
2 teaspoons ground cloves

Remove stems from grapes and wash thoroughly. Place in a large stewpan (do not add water) and slowly bring to a boil. Then simmer and stir until all grapes are broken. Put through a colander. Return to stewpan, stir in remaining ingredients, and simmer about 2 hours, stirring frequently.

Pour into sterilized jars and seal.

Tarragon Vinegar

Fresh tarragon
Vinegar

Gather fresh tarragon just before it blossoms. Bruise by twisting. Place in sterilized jars. Pour in enough vinegar to cover; let stand in a cool place for a couple of months. Then cork.

🐦   🐦   🐦

Dilled Okra Pickles

3   pounds whole young okra
    Celery leaves
6   garlic cloves
6   large heads dill (with stems)
1   quart water
1   pint white vinegar
½   cup salt

Scrub okra and pack into 6 sterlized pint jars with a few celery leaves, a garlic clove, and a head of dill for each jar. To pack neatly, put first layer in stem down and second layer point down.

Make a brine of water, vinegar, and salt—heat to boiling and pour over okra. Seal jars and let stand for 3 weeks.

Makes 6 pints.

Chow Chow

  2 heads cabbage
12 sweet green peppers
12 sweet red peppers
12 medium-sized onions
     Salt
     Sugar
  2 teaspoons mustard seed
  2 teaspoons celery seed
  2 teaspoons tumeric
     Vinegar

Finely chop cabbage, peppers, and onions; drain. Place in a large saucepan and season with salt and sugar. Stir in mustard seed, celery seed, and tumeric; cover with vinegar. Bring to a boil and boil gently for 20 minutes. Put in sterilized pint jars and seal.

❦   ❦   ❦

Bread and Butter Pickles

12 cucumbers, sliced fine
  4 onions, sliced
     Salt
  2 cups vinegar
  1 cup sugar
  1 teaspoon tumeric
  1 teaspoon mustard seed
  1 teaspoon celery seed

Layer cucumbers and onions in a large pan, sprinkling a little salt on each layer. Let stand one hour; drain.

Combine remaining ingredients in a large saucepan and cook until syrupy. Carefully add cucumbers and onions; let simmer for 5 minutes. While still hot, put in sterilized jars and seal.

Makes about 1 to 2 pints.

Preserved Watermelon Rind

2 cups diced watermelon rind
1 teaspoon salt
1 cup cider vinegar
2 cups sugar
1 3-inch cinnamon stick
8 cloves

Cover watermelon rind with water. Add salt and soak overnight. Drain and soak in fresh water for 2 hours; drain again.

Combine 1 cup water, cider vinegar, and sugar in a saucepan and bring to a boil. Tie cinnamon stick and cloves in a cheesecloth bag and drop in pan. Boil for 5 minutes. Stir in drained watermelon rind and boil for 30 minutes. Remove spice bag. Place rind in sterilized jars, cover with vinegar mixture, and seal jars.

Makes about 2 pints.

❧   ❧   ❧

Pinnacle Pickled Peaches

7 pounds peaches
  Whole cloves (3 to 4 per peach)
1 pint cider vinegar
6 cups sugar
2 cinnamon sticks, broken in pieces

Peel peaches and insert cloves. Combine cider vinegar, sugar, and cinnamon in a heavy pan; boil about 12 minutes. Drop in peaches and cook until tender but firm. Test with a straw.

Lift out peaches and place in sterilized jars. Continue cooking syrup until slightly thickened. Pour over peaches and seal immediately.

Tartar Sauce

1   cup mayonnaise
2   tablespoons chopped green onions
2   tablespoons chopped capers
2   tablespoons chopped parsley
1   tablespoon chopped pickle
1   teaspoon lemon juice

Thoroughly combine all ingredients; chill.
Makes about 1½ cups.

èa.   èa.   èa.

Quapaw Barbecue Sauce

½   pound butter
1   pint water
⅓   cup vinegar
1   teaspoon dry mustard
2   tablespoons sorghum (or brown sugar)
2   tablespoons Worcestershire sauce
1   teaspoon hot sauce
1   teaspoon black pepper
1   cup finely chopped onion
1   tablespoon paprika
1   tablespoon salt
2   tablespoons chili powder
½   teaspoon red pepper

Combine all ingredients in a saucepan and simmer for 40 minutes
to 1 hour; stir occasionally. Store in refrigerator.
Makes about 2 pints.

Mincemeat

1½ pounds lean beef, coarsely chopped
 2 quarts chopped apples
½ pound chopped suet
 1 pound raisins
 1 pound currants
¼ pound candied citron
¼ pound orange peel
¼ pound lemon peel
 2 cups apple cider
 1 cup grape juice
 3 cups brown sugar
1½ teaspoons salt
 2 tablespoons cinnamon
 1 teaspoon cloves
 1 teaspoon nutmeg

Boil beef in water to cover; drain and reserve 1 quart of broth. Combine meat and broth with all remaining ingredients and cook over low heat until apples are soft. Stir occasionally with a wooden spoon, being sure to stir down to the bottom of the pan.

Pack in sterilized jars or an earthen crock. Store in a cool place for at least 2 weeks before using.

Index

A

B

S

Y

Other Books From August House Publishers

First Ladies of Arkansas

The First Ladies of Arkansas chronicled by one of their number
with more than 130 Photographs.
Hardback $24.95 / ISBN 0-87483-091-5

The Southern Hospitality Cookbook

For those who want to enjoy the tradition
of Southern hospitality—but lack a mansion and a kitchen staff.
Paperback $11.95 / ISBN 0-87483-348-5

Southern Accent

A *Southern Living Hall of Fame* cookbook
collected by the Pine Bluff, Arkansas Junior League
Hardback $16.95 / ISBN 0-87483-376-0

Thirty Years at the Mansion

Recipes, recollections, and photographs from the Arkansas
Governors Mansion. "Recipes fit for a president."—USA Today.
Hardback $24.95 / ISBN 0-935304-88-6
Paperback $16.95 / ISBN 0-87483-135-0

August House Publishers
P.O. Box 3223, Little Rock, Arkansas 72203
1-800-284-8784